EXEMPLARS OF TEACHING METHOD

HARRY S. BROUDY
JOHN R. PALMER
University of Illinois

EXEMPLARS
OF
TEACHING METHOD

Rand McNally & Company
Chicago

Preface

This book is the outgrowth of an essay prepared for the *Handbook of Research on Teaching*, edited by N. L. Gage for the American Educational Research Association and published by Rand McNally & Company in 1963. This chapter in the *Handbook* was written by the senior author of this book and was entitled "Historic Exemplars of Teaching Method."

A number of colleagues suggested that the chapter be expanded and published separately so that it could be used as a supplement to systematic textbooks in the history of education and as a source of background materials in administration, curriculum, methods, and other standard courses in education.

Following these suggestions, permission was sought and received from the American Educational Research Association for the enlargement and separate publication of the work. The expansion took two forms. One was the addition of new material on Isocrates, Alcuin, Ascham, and Kilpatrick. The other expansion was internal. Large portions of the material were rewritten. Although no effort was made to write down to the student, an effort for which he is rarely grateful, we did keep in mind that this book was primarily for students whereas the original chapter was primarily for the eyes of research workers in education. Biographical notes were enlarged, terminology changed, arguments expanded and rephrased.

Although the rationale of the book is stated in Chapter I, it may not be superfluous to restate its purpose. This is not a book on the history of education; it has neither the scope nor the continuity to merit that honorable designation. It concentrates rather on teaching method as it was exhibited in the work of a few noted teachers. We regard the methods of these exemplars as related to the challenges presented to the schools by the cultural stresses of the periods in which they lived. We have, however, tried to make our hypotheses on these matters easy to discern, so that the critical powers of the student will not be inhibited. And if the student or his instructor is impelled by our

v

interpretations to institute historical studies to confirm or refute them, we shall regard this as a gain for all concerned.

We believe, in conclusion, that at a time when teaching and the preparation for teaching are under intense scrutiny from so many quarters, it may be helpful for prospective teachers, administrators, supervisors, and researchers to make the acquaintance of men who were "professional educators" in the best sense of both words. Our exemplars, without exception, looked on teaching as a mission, as a way of life. They were reflective as well as dedicated men, and they sensed and articulated the fact that in teaching, one touches the nerve of the process whereby life becomes human. With good teaching and fortunate circumstances, we achieve education, and the human life becomes the good life.

Teachers who write books are almost certain to have forgotten the many sources of their thoughts and words. We are no exceptions, and to attempt to list our benefactors among students and colleagues would only underscore the extent of our forgetfulness.

Special acknowledgment is due to the American Educational Research Association and to Rand McNally for permission to reproduce considerable portions of the material contained in Chapter 1 of the *Handbook of Research on Teaching,* edited by N. L. Gage (1963).

HARRY S. BROUDY
JOHN R. PALMER

Urbana, Illinois
February 1964

Table of Contents

Chapter I

INTRODUCTION

Once a society becomes self-conscious about the nurture of its young, the seed of educational theory is sown. Because men are anxious to control the educative process, they hypothesize as to how the outcomes they envision for their pupils can best be secured. As their observation becomes refined and their thinking more precise, educational practice ceases to be mechanically conventional or blindly empirical. The systematic concern with what to teach and how to teach it stimulates the growth of educational theory both among the professionals who apply it and among the laymen who, in all history, probably have never been completely satisfied with what schools do to and for their children.

What sort of educational theory will command interest during a given period of history? This depends on the type of learnings needed for success in that period. In an age when using the Latin tongue was crucial for the success of the courtier, the diplomat, and the churchman, educators speculated about methods of teaching Latin literature and composition. In our own age, when science and mathematics are richly rewarded, theorists strain to discover methods for the efficient teaching of these subjects, and should the time ever come when success depends on communication with space creatures, a spate of monographs, experiments, and doctoral theses that testify to an overwhelming preoccupation with this kind of learning will pour forth. Future historians, upon examing this outpouring, may pardonably conclude that during the era in question no other type of content and method existed.

These conjectures suggest that one way of understanding an era is to study the educational concerns distinctive of that era.

There are, however, some precautions to be observed. For example, history has not preserved the stories of all schools and all teachers. If we go by what has been preserved, can we be sure that it suitably represents what in fact existed? Would it not be tempting for a commentator in 2160 A.D. to conclude that in the 1960's in America the dominant pattern of higher education was that of Harvard, Yale, and Princeton; or that all elementary school children were enthusiastic about theoretical physics and axiomatic mathematics?

Perhaps we know enough about the course of Western civilization to hazard a few more conjectures as to what the literary and historical accounts are likely to preserve. One of these guesses, as has already been noted, is that in any period the schools will stress the skills, knowledge, and values that the dominant social group judges to be essential to its success. However, one can also be fairly sure that in any period a narrow view of success and a wider one will vie for support. In our own time, for example, the schools are under great pressure to provide manpower for industry, government, and the military establishment. To train men for such jobs is the response to an obvious and fairly immediate definition of success. A school that promises to provide the requisite skills and knowledge will be patronized, and if patronized by men of social power and prestige, will become "prestigious" and exclusive.

On the other hand, our times are not lacking for men who warn that success is more than vocational achievement; that the democratic commitment, moral integrity, and aesthetic enjoyment are also important, perhaps ultimately, more important than the rewards of the job. Let us call those who stress the wider view of success the advocates of virtue. The educational theory of a period will strive for a curriculum and methodology that promise to achieve both immediate success and long-range success in the form of a life of virtue, that is, a personality that is realizing its potentialities for human well-being.

This brings up another conjecture. Although history is likely to record the names and doings of only the more successful schools and teachers, one might suppose that in any period more or less faithful imitations of the successful institutions and their personnel existed. Since the most "prestigious" schools tend to become exclusive, these imitations provided second, and perhaps, third and fourth best alternatives for those who could not afford, or could not achieve, the best.

As a rule, one finds in these imitations, depending on their distance from the model, a greater emphasis on immediate success than on the broader conception of it. For one thing, pupils and parents excluded from the best may feel unsure about their status and be more anxious to secure external proofs of it via schooling. To such parents and students the skill and knowledge needed to do what the successful people are doing are more important outcomes than the less negotiable qualities of virtue. In such schools, general education, although admired and praised, tends to lose out to vocational training in the competition for curricular time and faculty attention.

Furthermore, one can be fairly sure, as Plato pointed out in the *Republic* (vi. 487–497) with respect to the philosophers, that the market for second-, third-, and fourth-rate schooling will be exploited by men who are themselves less than first rate. This is made all the more possible and likely when teaching is formalized and methodized, because the external procedures can then be replicated without cultivating the knowledge and character of the first-rate teacher.

The attempt to assess the importance of this or that form of schooling is further complicated by the fact that in retrospect we tend to exaggerate the influence of men who have become famous. Comenius, Pestalozzi, and Froebel are only a few of the schoolmen one could cite as examples of this tendency. All three had visions of the role of schooling that neither the schools nor the societies of their time shared. As a result, the innovations they urged probably could not readily have been found in the schools of their time, although the foreshortening effects of history give rise to the illusion that they were widespread. Thus, even today, many believe that by 1957 all American schools had adopted the practices advocated by the Progressive movement in education. Actually, the number of schools that operated on anything like a pure version of the activity curriculum or by the project method was very small.

The innovations are important for our purpose because they are signals of an attempt to meet a change in the success routes of the culture, and the new design for schooling may herald a change in content, method, or both. Thus, the shift from Latin language to science marked one of the great changes in the success patterns of Western culture, just as the shift from the study of rhetoric to theology marked another. In great teachers as in great artists, the old and the new commingle so as to express the essence of a passing era while, at the same time, pointing to the possibilities of the era to come.

Challenges to Schools

Because formal schools arise only when the culture of a group can no longer be transmitted adequately by the informal learnings that go on in the ordinary transactions of group living,[1] one can understand what schools are doing by noting the demands or challenges to which they are trying to respond, to use a phrase of Arnold Toynbee's.

In any society the groups that seek or possess power and prestige expect the schools to prepare the young to occupy the positions and play the roles that the parents occupy or would like to occupy. For this purpose, schooling has to teach the young in two dimensions. First, the schools are expected to instruct the young in the linguistic and other symbolic skills needed (a) for communication and (b) for retrieving the knowledge stored within the symbolic systems. Thus, for many centuries a knowledge of Latin and Greek was needed not only for international communication but also as a means of gaining access to the best knowledge available to the Western world. This is the cognitive dimension.

---

[1] Emile Durkheim (1956) notes that while all societies have some form of education, pedagogy appears only at a relatively advanced period in their history, i.e., when reflective thought is demanded by the social conditions. In a very stable society the teacher has little sense of the need to be guided by theory. It becomes a pressing concern, however, when intellectual and moral security are disturbed in times of rapid social change.

The second dimension is that of value. The preferences, attitudes, systems of priorities, and personality models of the dominant groups also have to be "sold" to the young. If the first dimension of study makes men successful, the second is designed to make them virtuous. So long as there is little doubt or diversity as to what "success" and "virtue" are to mean, the schools, although varying in quality, settle down to a fairly standard curriculum and teaching style. Once the current meanings of success and virtue are challenged, the school is also challenged.

Unfortunately, learning how to do this or that (skills), learning that this or that is the case (information), or learning why such and such is the case (explanations) presents one kind of task to the school, while learning to be a certain kind of person presents another kind. The school can control the important conditions governing the learning of arithmetic and geography. At the end of a given period of instruction one can give tests to find out whether the instruction was effective. Furthermore, what one means by arithmetic or geography is fairly clear to anyone interested in these fields of study.

On the other hand, becoming brave or temperate or wise, in short, becoming virtuous calls for the building of dispositions that are to lie in wait for an opportunity to be exercised throughout one's life. The conditions under which one becomes brave, temperate, and wise are not confined to the school. Certainly many men developed these virtues before there were schools, while some failed to develop them in the best of schools. Nor, finally, is it always clear as to just what courage, for example, shall mean. To the little child it means not crying in the face of certain obvious dangers such as barking dogs, the attacks of other children, dark rooms, and angry fathers. Later, questions arise about the bravery of risking mutilation by a strange and angry dog and whether or not retreating amid the jeers of one's fellows is not the *really* brave thing to do. Is there, then, a kind of knowledge that helps make men brave? Or does one just have to be brought up to be brave? Or is there some combination of knowledge and habit that the school can strive to bring about?

Accordingly, in every age, problems of curriculum and method orbit around the controversy between what one would now call general and special education. General education, as distinguished from vocational special education, is somehow supposed to fit us for the whole span of life, for the life of man as man. While it is also concerned with the kind of schooling that will help one to live life efficiently, it is primarily concerned with the kind of knowledge that promises to make man wise, the virtue that, according to Socrates, renders all the other virtues efficacious.

Hence, we find Socrates lecturing his pupils about the kind of knowledge which is virtue and thus, in a way, trying to stem their impetuous rush to secure another kind of knowledge, namely, vocational know-how; knowledge that by making them eloquent, would also make it possible for them to become successful politicians. The Rhetoricians, or the Sophists as they were called in Athens, provided, or at least promised to provide, training that would lead to success. The Athenian youth, not unlike youth in all subsequent ages, was torn between the fascination of the Greek ideal as represented by Socrates and the excitement and fame of public life. The conflict is one that we shall encounter in every age.

It is interesting to note that Socrates did not take up arms against other useful arts such as carpentry or navigation. Eloquence as an art was a somewhat different case, for it could be used in behalf of bad as well as good causes. To make a man eloquent was not necessarily to make him good. To be sure, carpentry and navigation could also be used for good or ill, but in the conduct of public affairs virtually no issue is morally indifferent, for by definition each affects the welfare of the state. The orator eloquent in behalf of evil causes represented to Socrates the greatest of social dangers.

In addition to this general challenge, there were more specific ones that elicited responses from formal schooling. After a period in which the learning of Greece and Rome was either blotted out or forgotten—and there were regions in which these ages were dark—how was one to go about restoring this learning? Charlemagne faced such a problem and assigned to Alcuin the task of finding a response to it (Chapter IV). Abelard responded to a somewhat more sophisticated challenge, namely, the reconciliation of the claims of human reason and religious authority on the minds of men. The restoration of the philosophy and logic of Aristotle presented problems to theologians that Scholasticism met in a distinctive way (Chapter V).

The further restoration of learning during the Renaissance, especially the restoration of the classical literatures as a source of knowledge and taste, was also a challenge to the schoolmaster. How were the classical languages to be taught to youngsters when rhetoric was no longer a "professional" subject, and Latin and Greek were no longer living languages? How was one to teach the glories of pagan literature without contravening the reservations entertained by the Christian religion on some of these glories? How was one to incorporate these diverse values and competences in the training of the successful man of affairs (Chapter VI)?

In the meantime, the physical sciences of astronomy, physics, chemistry, were coming to new life in a surge of theoretical activity. They offered a stimulus both to the intellectual and to the humanitarian yearnings of mankind. So did the exploration of new continents and the possibilities of new material resources and trade. To utilize these new developments, however, required learning about matters that were not to be found in the classical literatures or in the theological speculations of the Middle Ages, interesting and important as they were during those ages. It took a long time for the schools to hammer out an appropriate response to this challenge.

Still another type of challenge was thrust upon the schools when new conceptions of child development challenged the notions of the innate depravity of man. The problem of finding the secret of "natural" development of human powers from stage to stage is fascinating to the educator because he knows so well that in schooling nothing succeeds so well as cooperating with nature. In Comenius, Pestalozzi, Froebel, and Herbart (Chapters VII, VIII, IX, and X, respectively) we have attempts to meet this challenge. These men shaped their curriculum and teaching styles to take account of economic, political, and ideological forces that were making an impact on man and his place in the social order. They were responses to the general challenge as to the relation of success to virtue, but they were also responses to the changing ground rules of survival and success in a changing world.

In our own country, the schools have been confronted not only with the challenges already mentioned (or their historical consequences) but with some that are peculiar to our own history. One of these was the task of transforming large numbers of immigrants into literate citizens who would be loyal to the American version of democracy. Another challenge was maintenance or the restoration of community and the values of the democratic way of life in a society that was rapidly becoming urbanized and mechanized. Large cities destroy the network of relations that makes the life of a village communal (Chapter XI).

Currently, the schools are facing another demand. It is that of fashioning a curriculum and methodology that embody both the personal values of democratic citizenship and the intellectual competences that such citizens need in a mass society that is trying to make terms with nuclear power (Chapter XII).

Selecting Exemplars

Why were the men about to be discussed picked as exemplars, rather than so many others who might have been chosen? First of all, because each displayed a distinctive style of teaching. It would be difficult indeed to mistake Socrates for Isocrates or Abelard for Alcuin; second, each of the men chosen has been identified with education and formal instruction. Finally, they illustrated something more than a way of teaching. Each illustrated a way of life, a system of values, and a response to a cultural challenge. Their responses set the tone for responses in other men and other times.

Leaders who were teachers in the broad and figurative sense in which we apply the term to Moses, Jesus, Buddha, were not chosen. For one reason, their goals transcended learning and instruction. This is not to say that one could not learn much about teaching from them, but they were not conspicuously interested in the methods by which they achieved their results. The men chosen were interested in methods and often were articulate about them. They belonged to the tribe of professional teachers, not only in that teaching was their major life occupation, but also because the processes of teaching and learning seemed to them worthy of serious and specialized study.

Phases of Teaching Method

Method refers to a set of procedures that are carried out according to some rule. The rule prescribes that in a certain class of situations, for example, the teaching of reading, steps are to be taken in a certain sequence, and that the procedures are to use certain materials in certain ways at certain times. To know the rule is to know "how to" carry out the procedure; to have gone through the procedure many times not only helps to make sure that one knows the rule, but also that one can carry out the actions prescribed by it.

There are many methods of teaching and, for all we really know, there may be just as many methods of learning. The method of Socrates differs from that of a Jesuit schoolmaster or that of Pestalozzi. The method of an inspirational lecturer is rarely confused with the method of teachers who work through projects and committees. Nevertheless, the search for the universal method goes on; educational research continues to scrutinize the teaching act in order to discover the essential steps, their articulation one with another, and to determine whether one method is more effective than another (Gage, 1963).

Inevitably such scrutiny of the teaching act leads one to divide it into phases or steps that presumably occur regardless of the particular style of teaching. The following set is one such division that may facilitate the discussion and comparison of teaching exemplars described in this book.

1. *Preparation for instruction.* Regardless of teaching style, there is something for the teacher to do before he confronts the pupil. It may be gathering materials, making a lesson plan, looking over test scores, reviewing one's lecture notes, or simply

rehearsing in imagination how one will introduce a topic and what the pupils' response might be. Different strategies of teaching call for different forms of preinstructional preparation.

2. *Motivation.* All theories of instruction recognize the need to capture the attention of the learner, and the devices for doing this are too numerous to mention. One professor is reported to have discharged blank cartridges at irregular intervals during his lectures to discourage drowsiness among his students. Other teachers have tried to smuggle in drill through games, while the standard method of bribing the pupil with prizes, grades, and smiles is too familiar to need elaboration.

This phase of method has received more attention from students of pedagogy than any other. Why? Because the natural interests of the child so often do not coincide with those of his adult mentor. As the content of formal schooling becomes more abstract, more bookish, and more remote from the daily doings of children, it engages the natural interest of the learner less and less, and the search for devices to capture his attention indirectly becomes more intense.

At least, this has been the customary view of the matter, a view that is currently being challenged by the fact that, approached in a certain way, young children do become interested in mathematical and scientific problems. There is, however, no real contradiction there. For one thing, not all children are equally responsive to these approaches, and not every level of abstraction can be utilized in instruction with equal success at all age levels. Furthermore, the interest of the child in a mathematical puzzle or game may not be the same as that of an adult who thinks of mathematics as a discipline to be mastered as part of a complete education. Nevertheless, if it is true that children can become genuinely interested in theoretical tasks earlier than was once thought likely, then this can have a powerful effect on teaching method, especially in that phase of it which has to do with motivation and presentation of the task.

The readiness of the learner in terms of his interests and his background becomes part of the problem of motivational strategy. No teacher can escape it nor can he solve it once and for all, even for the same class or the same pupil. In the work of

William Heard Kilpatrick (Chapter XI) we shall examine a theory of teaching that boldly proposes to solve the problem of motivation by teaching only what is genuinely interesting to the learner, that is, an activity in which the learner can engage naturally. The motivating styles of Socrates, Froebel, and Herbart differ from each other and from that of Kilpatrick as well.

3. *Presentation of the learning task.* Once attention is captured, the teacher confronts the pupil with something to be done. It may be a problem to be solved, a passage to be read, something to be looked up, a question to be answered. The task may be performed forthwith or the next day; it may be simple or complicated. The important point, however, is that in presenting the task the teacher has to distinguish between what is given to the pupil in the way of cues and what is left for the pupil to do on his own. When the task is to imitate a demonstration by the teacher, e.g., forming the letter S in penmanship, or sounding a new word in foreign language, or performing a computation, the cues are numerous; when the task is an original problem, the cues may be few.

If the task is replication of an ideal response, the presentation takes the form of a demonstration of the response and the means of achieving it. Aside from skill learnings, not much school work is used replicatively. More often the teacher wants the pupil to rearrange ideas, make logical or artistic combinations of materials, fill in gaps in meaning, or even to create solutions to problems, samples of which are presented. Prior to the presentation the teacher decides upon the strategy to be used, and this depends on which elements in the presentation are to be replicated, which are to be interpreted, and which are to be applied. From here on, presentation is more like an art than a skill or a science; more like a stage performance than a planned procedure. Like the artist, the teacher bases each step on an intuition as to what the situation now requires, and with 25 individuals making individual responses or not responding at all, the teacher must rely on sensitivity and experience to sustain him from moment to moment.

4. *Inducement of the trial response.* Invariably the teacher prods the pupil to say or do something that will indicate how

successful the presentation has been. If the teacher has just demonstrated how to write the letter *m* or how to pronounce the word "cannibal," she will ask a member of the class to try the letter or the word. In a more complicated task, she may seek answers that tell her whether the meanings of such words as "zone," "river basin," and the like in a geography lesson are clear to the pupils. In brief, the trial response is literally that, an attempt to perform the assigned task with little or no practice; it is also an attempt that is not "for keeps." It is a response that guides pupil and teacher, but it is not one to which a grade is assigned. Yet this trial response or series of trial responses is indispensable, because the next step in the teaching tactics of the teacher depends on what is learned from it.

5. *Correction of the trial response.* Once in a while, the trial response is so good that no further instruction is necessary. In mathematics, for example, the pupil may grasp the reasoning involved in a problem on the first trial, and the lesson is over so far as he is concerned. Or a pupil with experience in reading grasps the meaning of a sentence or paragraph the first time around. Usually the first trial is not the last one. When this is the case, the teacher corrects the trial response, or says or does something that helps the pupil correct it. Even such remarks as "Yes, that is right" or "Are you sure that is what you mean?" are means of correcting the trial response. Much of the current interest in programed textbooks and teaching machines is due to the fact that they elicit the trial response and give clues for correcting it, and often do so far more efficiently than a live teacher can.

6. *Fixation of response.* Most of the time a learning is produced not for the moment but for an extended future. Procedures for fixing the response depend on how the learning is to be used. Drill, varied repetition, and repetition with reduced cues in varying contexts, all lead up to the moment when the teacher feels that no more time can or need be given to the learning task. Psychologists speak of "overlearning" certain responses, that is, practicing them well beyond a given level of competence. A response that is used over and over again also becomes overlearned, so that we never forget certain rhymes and stories

learned in very early childhood. However, many of the pupil's learnings will not be used repeatedly in life, and therefore we do not go to great pains to fix the response into a habit. Some of these learnings are allowed to become part of the pupil's "apperceptive mass" whereby his life and subsequent learnings are enriched. Often these dividends are collected by the pupil long after he has forgotten the original learning capital from which they are earned.

7. *Test response and evaluation.* The teacher elicits from the pupil the test response that with a minimum of cues brings forth the right answer or the appropriate procedures from the pupil, whereupon he passes judgments on the adequacy of the learning.

Many of the theories in education take their departure from one or more of these phases of method. How to reduce the gap between interests of the teaching and learning generations is a great mother of teaching theory, as can be seen in the work of such men as Comenius, Pestalozzi, Froebel, Herbart, Dewey, and Kilpatrick. Other theories have received their impetus from the problems of presentation and correction, especially when a change in subject matter made an older form of these activities inappropriate. This happened when science and mathematics had to be taught as conceptual systems rather than as statements to be memorized.

As success routes change from one era to another and the content of the curriculum becomes shaped to the new requirements, method is also affected. The phases of method outlined above all remain, but the procedures followed are modified. Presentation when the learning task is to appreciate an ode by Horace is a different procedure from presentation when the learning task is to learn to operate a lathe. However, certain objectives remain fairly constant regardless of changes in success routes. Among these are the symbolic skills, the basic ideas, and the basic value commitments of the culture. Methods for teaching these outcomes are, therefore, a perennial concern of the educational theorist today just as it was of the men included in this study (Broudy, 1961, Chapter 14).

A word or two should be said in this introductory chapter

about the relation between the descriptions of teaching exemplars and the history of education or, more particularly, the history of teaching.

Although some effort is made to provide a setting for the discussion of each exemplar, the accounts are not, strictly speaking, historical. No attempt is made, for example, to include all the important teachers of a period. Nor is any systematic attempt made to relate one period to another or one theory to another in terms of what caused what. For this kind of discussion histories of education or of teaching should be consulted. In this volume the authors are primarily concerned with conveying something of the teaching style of the exemplars and how their teaching reflected or exemplified the pedagogical problems of their age.

Chapter *II*

THE RHETORICIANS,
FATHERS OF METHOD

Rhetorical education, as we shall have occasion to note, flour-
ishes whenever success depends upon ability to speak effectively. Such periods tend to coincide with political democracy
when decisions are made by juries, legislative bodies, or even
mobs; in short, when the power to sway an audience can be
turned into political power. Small wonder that in early Greece
and later in republican Rome teachers of rhetoric were popular
and often prosperous. These teachers were eager to find a method
for doing their work efficiently or, at least, for keeping up with
their rivals in the field.

Effective oratory sways the hearer either by argument or by
arousing his emotions. The cogency of argument depends on the
weight and exploitation of the evidence. Sympathy and antipathy
depend on the way language is used to evoke anger, pity, hatred,
and love with respect to the person or proposal under discussion.
(Against the passions aroused by his accusers, the cogency of
Socrates' argument did not prevail.) Accordingly, the training of
the orator had to provide (a) means of securing evidence, (b)
skill in argument, (c) facility with the evocative or emotive use
of language, and (d) a practical command of social psychology.

Sometimes the evidence had to be dug out of the circumstances surrounding the case at issue. If it were a case of alleged
treason, for example, the advocate would have to find out
whether his client did or did not meet with agents of the enemy,
take bribes, and divulge secrets of state. Often, however, the
advocate's job was to show that his client's action was like that
of some historic figure who was acclaimed as a benefactor of the
state rather than condemned as a traitor. Inasmuch as all histories

and literatures are rich in stories of real and alleged treason, to know these sources was also to have access to an important kind of evidence.

It was a kind of evidence, one might say, that combined both the content and the form of an argument, an argument by analogy. The content consisted of the points at which the accused and the famous historic personage were alike and the circumstances of their actions the same. The argument consisted of persuading the listener that the judgment passed upon the accused should be the same as that which had been passed upon the hero.

The use of literary sources guaranteed an emotionally rich and evocative flow of language. The quotations from poetry and drama would be rich in imagery and could easily arouse in the audience the associations that a shrewd speaker would find advantageous for his purpose. Indeed, the literature would also afford him good samples of social psychology: of how in days gone by Rhetoricians had swayed juries and assemblies by dramatic maneuvers and surprising revelations. It was not merely the skill of speaking or speech writing that constituted the professional armament of the Rhetorician, but also a flexible command of the literature that formed a common background of ideas, images, and feelings for those who would take part in the rhetorical occasion.

When, therefore, a Sophist of the fifth century B.C., a forerunner of the Rhetoricians, promised to undertake the training of a young man for three or four years and guaranteed to make of him a successful man of affairs for a fee of 10,000 drachmas, as did Protagoras of Abdera (Marrou, 1956), how did he propose to redeem the promise? Presumably by training him in the skills of speaking, but also by providing him with the resources for speaking—a rich fund of legend, history, and literature.

Protagoras

In order to get students, the ancient Sophist had to advertise himself and his wares. Having no permanent school, he traveled from town to town setting up a temporary base of operations at some house or hall. There he gave a sample lecture on some topic suggested by the audience, or improvised an oration on a theme of his own choosing.

A classic description of such a session is given in Plato's dialogue *Protagoras*. While it was still dark, Hippocrates, an excited young man, roused Socrates from sleep to tell him that three famous Sophists—Protagoras (485–415 B.C.), Hippias of Elis, and Prodicus of Ceos (both living in the fifth century B.C.)—had arrived in Athens and were at the house of the wealthy citizen Callias. Hippocrates wanted Socrates to introduce him to Protagoras and to persuade the famous Sophist to accept him as a pupil.

They were not the first to arrive at the Callias residence. Protagoras was walking in the portico followed by a "train of listeners" who accompanied him on his travels and a group of distinguished Athenians. In another lobby, Hippias was discoursing on astronomy, while a third knot of admirers surrounded Prodicus, who was still in bed. In the dialogue it is remarked that one could not make out what Prodicus was saying but that he spoke with a booming sound.

Protagoras contains the typical ingredients of the sample lecture: the myth and its interpretation; proof by argument; and the reading or reciting of a Homeric poem or legend together with critical commentaries on it. Several points about these set speeches should be noted: First, they were samples of what the pupil would himself produce on future occasions, i.e., a kind of work sample. Second, requiring a student to reproduce a speech by the master was a major method of teaching eloquence. In the Platonic dialogue *Phaedrus,* for example, Socrates asks Phaedrus to repeat to him the speech he had heard from Lysias.

> PHAEDR. What do you mean, my good Socrates? How can you imagine that my unpractised memory can do justice to an elaborate work, which the greatest rhetorician of the age spent a long time in composing. . . .
>
> Soc. I believe that I know Phaedrus about as well as I know myself, and I am very sure that the speech of Lysias was repeated to him, not once only, but again and again;—he insisted on hearing it many times over and

Lysias was very willing to gratify him; at last, when nothing else would do, he got hold of the book, and looked at what he most wanted to see,—this occupied him during the whole morning;—and then when he was tired of sitting, he went out to take a walk, not until, by the dog, as I believe, he had simply learned by heart the entire discourse, unless it was unusually long, and he went to a place outside the wall that he might practise his lesson.[1]

Third, Homer and other poets were used both as authorities on matters of policy and for literary appeal. The Sophists did not ignore other sources of knowledge; they had specialists in mathematics, astronomy, art, and all the other branches, because the legislator who might have to discourse on any topic needed a wide variety of information. Nevertheless, it was literature that celebrated the ethos of the time, and it was the medium in which speaker and audience most readily achieved communion (Jaeger, 1943, II, 107 ff.).

Isocrates

The Sophists of the fifth century aimed at two rather distinct lines of activity: the study of rhetoric and the ideal of an encyclopaedic education. The first was obviously a practical kind of schooling for the public life of the developing democratic cities, where political power was the reward of the orator who could guide and control the deliberation of a public meeting. Encyclopaedic knowledge was the Sophist's answer to the demand for a broader education to meet the requirements of a changing and more complex life. In the fourth century, Isocrates eminently combined these two forms of education both in his life and in his school.

Isocrates' (436–338 B.C.) formative years paralleled the great political and social crises marking the decline of Athenian power after the disastrous Peloponnesian War. He saw rhetorical instruction as a means by which to reform and rejuvenate the

---

[1]From *The Dialogues of Plato* by B. Jowett (4th ed.), 1953, III, 134, by permission of The Clarendon Press for the Jowett Copyright Trustees.

state through the education of statesmen capable of dealing with the challenges of the post-war period. To accomplish this, rhetoric had to find an ideal which could be ethically edifying but which could also be effective at the level of practical political action. Isocrates thought he had found it in Panhellenism (the unification of the Greek states), to which he was able to give both an ethical and a practical dimension.

If Isocrates ever wrote a detailed account of his teaching procedure, it has not survived. However, a good deal can be reconstructed from his literary works. The earliest surviving written statement suggesting that imitating one's elders and betters helps a student to improve whatever ability he has is that of Isocrates. In *Against the Sophists* (1929, 17–18) he asserts that the teacher must not only expound the principles of the art, but

> must in himself set such an example of oratory that the students who have taken form under his instruction and are able to pattern after him will, from the outset, show in their speaking a degree of grace and charm which is not found in others (1929, 17–18).
>
> In this process, master and pupil each has his place; no one but the pupil can furnish the necessary capacity; no one but the master, the ability to impart knowledge; while both have a part in the exercises of practical application; for the master must painstakingly direct his pupil, and the pupil must rigidly follow the master's instruction (Isocrates, *Antidosis*, 1928, 188).[2]

The following passage from the *Antidosis* (183–185), comparing the training of the mind to that of the body, suggests his general procedure:

> For when they take their pupils in hand, the physical trainers instruct their followers in the postures which have been devised for bodily contests, while the teachers of philosophy impart all the forms of discourse in which the mind expresses itself. Then, when they have made them familiar and thoroughly conversant with these lessons, they set them at exercises, habituate them to work,

---

[2] Reprinted by permission of Harvard University Press.

and require them to combine in practice the particular things which they have learned, in order that they may grasp them firmly and bring their theories into closer touch with the occasions for applying them. . . . Watching over them and training them in this manner, both the teachers of gymnastic and the teachers of discourse are able to advance their pupils to a point where they are better men and where they are stronger in their thinking or in the use of their bodies. However, neither class of teachers is in possession of a science by which they can make capable athletes or capable orators out of whomsoever they please.

It is significant that Isocrates shifts quickly from the purely rhetorical side of his instruction to the preparation which it gives for practical life. This practical aim of all his teaching is shown indirectly in the passages in which he condemns other studies. Eristic, astronomy, and geometry are useful studies, particularly as a preparation for "philosophy," but they are despised by the average man because they have no practical value, no connection with life (*Antidosis*, 1928, 262).

Isocrates' method of instruction may be divided into three parts. The first was instruction in "ideas"—the thought elements, the styles or manners of presentation, the general principles or theories behind composition and speech. The forms or ideas were the intellectual counterparts of the positions of the body taught by the gymnastic instructor. Teaching of rhetoric began with the analysis of speech into these fundamental patterns. The second part of the method was the presentation and analysis of models or exemplary speeches, while the third consisted in weaving the learning products of the first two phases together to form a speech appropriate to the requirements of a given situation or subject, a process requiring much study and practice.

How Isocrates presented the first part can be inferred from certain of his own discourses. Occasionally he used peculiarly short, disconnected passages, almost in the form of proverbs, in a style quite different from that which he usually employed. In the form in which he presented them to his pupils, these items were a collection of ideas on such topics as government, private morality, and the qualifications and duties of a general that his students could memorize and use.

Learning the technique of rhetoric was comparatively easy, Isocrates contended, if the aspirant studied with the right man, but the correct use of the technique could not be brought under any set of rules or taught by one man to another—it could only be learned by experience. The future orator must try the effect of each arrangement and combination of technique on the audience, and so draw up his own system (*Antidosis*, 91–93). The audience for these trials was provided by other pupils of the school, with the master as chief critic. Pupils and master joined in careful analysis and criticism of their own creative efforts, continually seeking to improve the effectiveness of their discourses (*Panathenaicus*, 1928, 229; *Areopagiticus*, 1928, 57–59; *To Philip*, 1928, 17–23). Although everyone took part, a good master was essential. By his personal influence he was able to communicate those finer elements of style which could not be conveyed in formal teaching. If he had taught well, all his pupils bore the stamp of his manner. Isocrates increased the probability of this happening by supplying his students with models of his own written speeches for study, analysis, and emulation.

In preparing their speeches, the pupils were to apply the rules they had learned and to reflect the more subtle influences that they had absorbed from their teacher. But they had also to think out the subject matter, and in this lay much of the merit of the system. The speeches were to be models not only of form but of content, not only of rhetorical skill but also of character, for Isocrates conceived the two to be inseparable. The contemplation of what was noble, for example, was a greater incentive to virtue than any so-called science of ethics. Moreover, since the orator's best argument was a good reputation, the young student needed to improve his conduct and character as much as possible. The practice of weighing just what thoughts and actions were suitable to the speech involved the faculty of sound deliberation which was vital to the formation of right judgment. Undoubtedly this very demanding creative effort, when coupled with the criticism provided by the master and the other pupils and repeated continuously over the three- or four-year training period, contributed significantly to the pupil's learning. Although in succeeding centuries instruction in rhetoric was often carried out by means of a fixed or traditional set of topics or problems, Isocrates much preferred that his students learn while attempting to resolve political or moral questions of genuine public concern at the moment.

As an aged man defending his life's work, Isocrates presented his written speeches as perfect classics to be imitated. Because the final inspiration of the pupil was derived from the work of the master himself, it is clear that imitation was the central principle of his teaching method (*Against the Sophists*, 1928, 9–18; *Antidosis*, 185). As a teacher, Isocrates apparently had great influence on his pupils, establishing a close personal bond in the true sense of the master-pupil relationship. This was possible in part because he had no more than five to nine pupils under his direction at any time (Marrou, 1956, p. 86), but more particularly because he developed the technique of classroom practice to a high level of proficiency. His ability as a teacher was verified by the large number of prominent persons who benefited from his tutelage over a teaching career spanning five decades. Crucial to his effectiveness was undoubtedly the close personal relationship that developed between master and pupil, a spiritual bond so intimate and powerful that it was frequently maintained throughout the life of both parties. The notion of a lecture hall filled with hundreds or even dozens of rapt or dozing listeners was completely foreign to his method. The characteristic teaching situation was a tutorial session between a teacher and one pupil, a situation that has become increasingly rare in today's movements toward mass education. It is not surprising that Isocrates was suspected of corrupting youth (*Antidosis*, 1928, 30) for he fully intended to influence their thought and actions, particularly with reference to political affairs. He hoped the ideas he fostered through his teaching would influence society by molding the characters of great leaders who could transform society.

Educational Theory and Rhetoric

It is one thing to deliver a brilliant sample speech to bewitch eager young men and another to deliver 10,000 drachmas worth of instruction. To accomplish the latter the Sophists needed a systematic organization of the materials to be taught and an orderly sequence of activities for teaching them.

By analyzing poetry and other instances of good writing and speaking, the Sophists were able to formulate rules for effective speaking and writing. Protagoras is credited with stating the rules for distinguishing the tenses of verbs and for classifying modes of utterance. Prodicus of Ceos studied synonyms in an attempt to clarify the meanings of words. Gorgias of Leontini (483–375 B.C.) is said to have devised the Gorgiac figures of antithesis, balance of clauses, and final assonance (Freeman, 1907; Gomperz, 1912; Marrou, 1956; Moore, 1936).

The analysis of materials and their recombination into teaching form had to be undertaken by the Sophists in every field they undertook to teach: etymology, geography, natural history, genealogy, laws of meter and rhythm, history, mythology, politics, ethics, criticism of religion, mnemonics, logic, tactics, strategy, music, drawing, painting, sculpture, and athletics.

In logic especially the Sophists had to make a beginning by analyzing rules of debate and argument. Protagoras is said to have formulated eristic, a debating method in which one takes a point conceded by an opponent and uses it as a starting point for further argument. Protagoras' Antilogies were, in a sense, the forerunners of the Socratic dialectic.

By 166 B.C., Dionysius of Thrace had formalized the steps to be followed in presenting a lecture on a literary work:

1. Give the selected passages an exact reading with respect to pronunciation, punctuation, and rhetorical expression.
2. Explain the figures of speech.
3. Explain the historical and mythological references.
4. Comment on the choice of words and their etymology.
5. Point out the grammatical forms employed.
6. Estimate the literary merit of the selection.

This established the form and style of the famous prelection and *exposition de texte* as a mode of instruction, but the point to be noted is that teaching method begins with analysis of the teaching act into a sequence of steps. The Sophists are rightly called the ancestors of the teaching profession, not only because they taught for fees but because they became self-conscious about teaching as an art, and this of necessity led them to the consideration of method.

Even in these days of carefully worked-out course syllabi it would be difficult to match the minuteness of analysis that went into the teaching of rhetoric in the schools of Greece and Rome.[3]

By the fourth century B.C., it was pretty well agreed by Aristotle and others that the teaching of rhetoric involved three factors: nature, art, and exercise. Then as now, teachers could only wish for a high order of innate talent and docile temperament. Hence, most of the attention had to be given to art and exercise.

By art (techné) the ancients had in mind something akin to what we mean by method, especially if the method were justified by principles or knowledge. From these principles one could derive definitions, rules, and precepts, very much as rules and procedures in carpentry or even in engineering and medicine are nowadays derived from certain sciences. Unfortunately, the learning of these rules by rote was regarded by generations of schoolmasters as equivalent to understanding the principles from which they were derived.

Exercise was the term applied to practice both in memorizing the rule and in applying it to sample tasks. In rhetoric, exercise consisted largely of imitating the best models available to the instructor. Inasmuch as the rules and precepts were derived from the type of poetry or speeches that were also to be used in the imitative exercise, rule and example coincided more often than might be the case if one were to apply the rules to modern literature and poetry. Thus, the method was reduced

---

[3] We have borrowed extensively from Clark's *Rhetoric in Greco-Roman Education* (New York: Columbia University Press, 1957) to indicate the great detail to which the analysis of both the subject matter and the methodology were carried.

to memorizing the rule and imitating selected models until the style of the model became "natural" for the pupil.

An idea of the complexity of the subject can be gained by noting that the art of speaking, and writing as well, was divided by Cicero (*De partitione oratoria*, 46 B.C.; Clark, 1957, pp. 69 ff.) into the following tasks:

inventio: to find out what one should say
dispositia: to arrange what one has found
elecutio: to clothe it with language
memoria: to secure it in one's memory
pronuntiatio: to deliver it

So much for the resources needed by the speaker. As to the oration or speech itself, six divisions were recognized:

exordium: opening
narratio: statement of the facts colored to favor the speaker's argument
divisio: forecast of main points the speaker plans to make
confirmatio: the argument in favor of the speaker's contentions
confutatio: rebuttal of possible objections
peroratio: conclusion or summation

Within these large divisions were numerous subdivisions. Cicero classified 17 sources of arguments for the *inventio*. As to style, Cicero came to be the model *par excellence*, but models also were sought in other standard Roman authors: Virgil, Horace, Ovid, Lucan, Statius, Persius, Martial, Catullus, Juvenal, and Sallust. Clark quotes Marrou to the effect that Latin was taught as a dead language as early as the days of Jerome and Augustine (Clark, 1957, p. 86; Marrou, 1938, p. 14).

The actual teaching procedure both in the school of the grammarian (for younger boys) and in the higher school of the rhetors was as follows:

1. The pupil would memorize the definitions, classifications, and rules as embodied in textbooks.
2. The teacher would analyze the models to be imitated by a prelection.
3. The pupil was directed to apply the precepts and imitate

the model in practice declamations or compositions on hypothetical themes.

The imitation, which was the heart of the method, was obviously not a simple duplication of the model. Good imitation involved:

1. Giving the student the results of careful study of the model by the teacher to reveal how the author achieved his effects. This analysis was offered by the teacher either in a lecture or by assigning material covering this point in a textbook (cf. Quintilian *Institutio*, II, v. 6–16).

2. Asking the student to write sentences that exhibited the stylistic characteristics of the model: periodic sentences, certain figures of speech, etc. Exercises in imitation included learning by heart, learning by translation from Greek to Latin, and paraphrasing poetry into prose.

Even the exercises in the earlier phases of composition study were not left to chance. There were collections of graded exercises (*progymnasmata*) to guide the writing and speaking practice. Other exercises called for retelling fables, plausible fictions, and stories from history; narrations dealing with persons; amplifying proverbs into a moral essay; refuting an argument; taking a set of facts typical of a class of situations and applying them to a particular case; praising or dispraising a thing or person (one writer treated of this exercise alone in 36 divisions and subdivisions); making comparisons; composing imaginary speeches that might have been given by some historical or mythological figure; describing objects and events vividly; arguing on set questions (e.g., Should a man marry?); and speaking for or against a piece of legislation.

This type of training has long been condemned as highly artificial and formal. In later centuries it deserved many of the hard things said about it, especially when oratory and elegant writing no longer served any significant social purpose. As a method, however, it had its merits.

Virtues and Shortcomings

In the first place, the method had the virtue of definiteness. At any given moment the pupil had little doubt as to what was expected of him, how he should go about it, and how well he was getting along. As a youngster in the grammar school, he might not be enthusiastic about memorizing definitions he did not understand or the endless writing of dull themes. Wise schoolmasters such as Quintilian understood this and used praise and reproof rather than harsh punishments as a means of class control. Yet routine and clarity of expectation contribute much to psychological security of the pupil and perhaps to the security of the teacher as well. If the teacher cannot be inspired, he ought to be at least intelligent, and if not that, at least methodical, but if he is not even methodical, all is lost. Provided he was not mired in the bewildering classifications and sub-classifications, the teacher could always know what to do next and, after a fashion, provide a reason to himself and to his pupil for doing it.

The reliance on habituation was almost complete. Quintilian believed that the pupil could form habits of premeditation and even of improvisation. He therefore advised: Have a good stock of thoughts and phrases available. If you have practiced the style of the speech and the order of presentation, you can think ahead of the audible words. However, the best form of exercise of improvisation is to speak daily before an audience of several persons, or to go over the speech silently, but forming the words. Above all, counseled Quintilian, keep writing: "We must write, therefore, whenever possible; if we cannot write, we must meditate: if both are out of the question, we must still speak in such a manner that we shall not seem to be taken unawares nor our client to be left in the lurch" (Quintilian *Institutio*, X, vii. 29).[4]

Though formal and rigid, the method provided for flexibility in at least two ways. For one thing, the goal of the instruction was to give the prospective speaker a set of standardized models for the kind of speaking occasions most likely to occur, e.g., the encomium, pleading a case, or urging legislation. Having perfected these speech- or essay-types, he could discharge any specific task merely by filling in the blanks with the right names and circumstances.

[4] Reprinted by permission of Harvard University Press.

Naturally, judgment and acumen would be needed to adjust the speech nicely to the occasion; even the Rhetoricians realized that there was no way of teaching this systematically. But by learning speech-types the pupil was acquiring flexibility. For example, if the accused had committed a crime that could be brought under the general heading of treason, the well-trained orator had at his disposal a whole store of remarks that could be made on treason: a nest of historical examples, appropriate quotations from the poets and mythology, as well as the utterances of noted men. Moreover, he had probably practiced the "treason" speech often enough to have a go at this one with a high degree of confidence.

A second type of flexibility was provided by the very rigidity of the method. By memorizing a large number of speech-types the future Rhetorician could reduce the amount of thinking he would have to do in a particular situation. Instead of having to figure out what he should do in terms of principles and rules, he could recognize the new situation as just like one he had practiced. In educational theory the utilizing of general principles to deduce solutions for particular situations is called transfer by generalization, whereas solving a new problem by replicating an old solution is called transfer by "identical" elements. Transfer by identical elements, if the elements are sufficiently well practiced, occurs in many instances when transfer by generalization does not, and for the duller pupils to whom generalization and abstraction are not easy, this is a great boon.

The methods of the rhetor also bring out the role of apprentice teaching or internship training. Because all the exigencies of the concrete speech-making situation could not be anticipated, the student was to select some orator to follow about and imitate. In the law courts and at public occasions, he was to listen to him and then write out his own speeches for the very same cases and occasions (Quintilian *Institutio*, X, v. 19–21). This is a recognition that all professional work is an art as well as a science; that sooner or later the professional operates at the level of the particular. The concrete situation—the sick patient, the unruly classroom, the courtroom tension, the crowd gathered at the funeral—cannot be verbalized without destroying some of the concreteness. Hence all professional training has to be crowned by practice under a master. This the Rhetoricians realized, as did the universities later on, when the student to a large extent learned by teaching.

Finally, the method presupposed that standards of excellence in speaking, writing, and thinking had already been achieved in the speaking, writing, and thinking of real or fictional characters in the past. It was a choice between denying the greatness of these products or copying them. Thus Quintilian said:

> Is it not sufficient to model our every utterance on Cicero? For my own part, I should consider it sufficient, if I could always imitate him successfully. But what harm is there in occasionally borrowing the vigor of Caesar, the vehemence of Caelius, the precision of Pollio or the sound judgment of Calvus? (*Institutio*, X, ii. 25).

Collections of model speeches were compiled and presumably used, e.g., *The Declamations of Quintilian,. Being an Exercitation of Praxis upon His XII Books, concerning The Institution of the Orator* (London, printed by F.R. for John Taylor, 1686). Isocrates also furnished speech models in his *Against the Sophists, Antidosis,* and *Panegyricus,* although they were not written solely for this purpose. Lazarus Piot's *The Orator: Handling a Hundred Several Discourses, in forme of Declamations* is a later sample (Clark, 1957, p. 261).

Imitation is a bad word in contemporary educational language. The abuses of imitation, when speaking and writing degenerated into empty exercises in form, contributed to its bad reputation. Nevertheless, as a method of teaching, imitation has to be evaluated apart from the uses and abuses to which it has been put. Can teaching wholly dispense with it? It is difficult to imagine a test of learning that does not compare the pupil's performance with a model of some sort. Sooner or later the language used by the pupil is compared with that of the scientist, historian, or geographer. If he speaks the way the models do, one hopes that he thinks the way they do. If he does not speak as they do, one doubts that he thinks as they do. One cannot be sure in either case, but the doubt is far greater in the latter situation than in the former.

However, there is a difference between using a model for the testing of learning and using duplication of a model as a means of teaching. In rhetorical education, as described above, exact duplication of material was demanded, especially in the early stages of training, but the final objective could not be exact replication. After all, the case before the court and the trainee was not the case Cicero (the model) had argued. The speaker had to make adjustments to the individuating features of the occasion. What he imitated, therefore, was the *form* of the speech after making a judgment as to which form was appropriate. He had a multitude of formulae from which to choose; he did not have to invent them as he went along. The formulae took care not only of the subject matter, but also of the style of composition and delivery. One could, therefore, reduce the art of speaking to a fairly mechanical sequence of selecting and imitating a model. However, mastery in any type of learning means having enough formulae on hand to meet a wide variety of circumstances with a minimum of judgment. Even the complicated reasoning of an engineer, physician, judge, or philosopher approximates this pattern as mastery is achieved (Smith & Ennis, 1961, Chapter 5).

Advocates of rhetorical methods no doubt believed that they were training memory, observation, imagination, and reasoning as well as forming specific skills. Their methods, unlike those advocated by the doctrines of formal discipline, did not rely on one or two subject matters to train these powers; nor were they indifferent as to what content was used for training. Formal discipline in rhetorical education was literally a discipline of forms, rather than a training of faculties. It relied on a rich stock of interchangeable formulae, not on the strengthening of certain powers. As to creativity, the method did not preclude imaginative maneuvering within the formulae; it encouraged it. The speaker's inventiveness was limited, however, to the turn of phrase or the phrasing of an argument. He was not expected to achieve new solutions to problems, and the method of his schooling did not provide for his learning to produce them (Clark, 1951; McKeon, 1936).

Chapter *III*

SOCRATIC METHOD

It was pointed out in a previous chapter that side by side with the schooling for immediate success a type of education tends to operate which aims at more general goals, goals that we have called virtue. Socrates, the teacher of Plato and the most famous of martyrs for the freedom of inquiry and teaching, is an eminent example of a teacher whose educational objective was virtue, rather than immediate political success. One of the exciting questions of his day was "Can virtue be taught?" This question got its point from the fact that the formula and method for teaching it were so elusive. As for the Sophists' claims that they were teaching virtue, Socrates showed them again and again that they could not even define virtue, and that what they were teaching was a set of skills that at best could only provide for immediate success.

The conflict between immediate success and virtue was especially crucial in the time of Socrates and Plato, because worldly success so largely depended on political activity. Although the best of the Rhetoricians claimed that they taught eloquence in order to help justice triumph, in practice it was the skill in argument rather than the justice of the cause that determined the excellence and success of the orator. We have a somewhat analogous situation today with atomic scientists themselves becoming sensitive to the uses of scientific knowledge. Physicists are still rated not on their moral virtue but rather on their ability as physicists, and the problem of their virtue is as much unsolved as was the problem of the virtue of the orator in the days of democratic Athens.

There were those like Xenophon who attacked the Sophists for their fee-taking and their flamboyant claims, and charged that they were innovators leading the youth away from the ancient virtues (*areté*). But Plato's criticism as expressed in many of his dialogues raised a more serious objection.

In the person of Socrates, the protest took the following form: In order to teach virtue, as the Sophists claimed to do, they would have to know what virtue really was. Yet on questioning them, Socrates found that instead of a definition of virtue, his respondents were likely to give him examples of conduct conventionally called virtuous. In the early P'atonic dialogues, for example, *Laches, Euthyphro*, and the *Menò*, Socrates is portrayed as trying to arrive at a generic definition of virtue or excellence.

Although no definition is achieved, each dialogue hints that knowledge is a common element in all the virtues. Virtue, Socrates argued, was a kind of knowledge, but knowledge of what? It was not like knowledge of the stars or common-sense knowledge of the world. To say that it was knowledge about the norms or standards of conduct is not satisfactory either, because it was obvious that men who knew what they ought to do nevertheless often failed to do it, or did what they acknowledged they ought not to have done, and virtue, if it was knowledge, was action-knowledge. In short, more than ordinary cognition was involved. Schooling for virtue meant shaping the whole personality in such a way that the standards of the good, true, and beautiful became a functional part of the individual's decision-making behavior. These standards were not only known but felt as compelling, and compelling because of their rightness rather than because of the social pressure behind them.

Now to impart this sort of education was a far cry from teaching boys how to make good speeches. How could it be brought about? In the works of Plato four methods can be distinguished: exhorting the learner to become concerned about the importance of his achieving these norms; dialectical self-examination; disciplining one's appetites (self-mastery); and a course of intellectual training culminating in dialectics. The first two of these approaches seem to have been characteristic of Socratic teaching; the latter two probably reflect Plato's own elaborate plan for the ideal state and the ideal guardian of that state as set forth in the *Republic*. The real Socrates did not, according to Xenophon, think so highly of mathematical knowledge as did the Platonic Socrates (Jaeger, 1943, II, 304).

Socratic Exhortation

In the *Apology*, Socrates said:

> Men of Athens . . . while I have life and strength I shall never cease from the practice and teaching of philosophy, exhorting any one whom I meet and saying to him after my manner: You, my friend . . . are you not ashamed of heaping up the greatest amount of money and honor and reputation, and caring so little about wisdom and truth and the greatest improvement of the soul, which you never regard or heed at all? [1]

The frequent use of exhortation to become concerned about the state of one's values (one's soul) has been noted by Jaeger (1943, II, 39). It is illustrated in the *Protagoras* (313 a-c) when Socrates, accompanying Hippocrates to the house of Callias to hear Protagoras, asks the excited young man,

> Well, but are you aware of the danger which you are incurring? If you were going to commit your body to some one, who might do good or harm to it, would you not carefully consider and ask the opinion of your friends and kindred, and deliberate many days as to whether you should give him the care of your body? But when the soul is in question, which you hold to be of far more value than the body, and upon the good or evil of which depends the well-being of your all—about this you never consulted either with your father or with your brother or with any of us who are your companions. But no sooner does this foreigner appear, than you instantly commit your soul to his keeping (IV, 137–138).

The learner had to be jolted into uneasy anxiety about his soul, just as contemporary man must be scared a bit before he trots off to his periodic medical checkup. Socrates was a past

---

[1] From *The Dialogues of Plato* by B. Jowett (4th ed.) 1953, I, 354, by permission of The Clarendon Press for the Jowett Copyright Trustees.

master of irony and the enigmatic statement. His partner in the dialogue was never sure how literally Socrates was to be taken. He was a provoker and a gadfly, especially to those who were well satisfied with themselves. His apparent quibbling over words infuriated his opponents.

Socrates usually began with a casual question about something his victim regarded as beyond question: the nature of courage, temperance, or justice. To be shown that one really did not know what seemed so certain, that one's common-sense definitions led to awkward consequences, and that one was, in short, abysmally ignorant precisely where one thought himself to be wise, elicited chagrin, embarrassment, and often anger— usually with Socrates, but occasionally with oneself. When the latter happened, the time was ripe for the positive side of the method, namely, dialectical self-examination.

The resemblance of Socrates' approach to that of the psychoanalyst is striking, and considering the relation of young men to their sponsors in the Greek scheme of things, the analogy is strong indeed. The notion of teaching as a species of love-therapy is an old one, and one that is peculiarly appropriate to what is called character training. It is, however, not restricted to it. Scholars and teachers welcome and, on occasion, even demand, discipleship from their students. The teacher in this relationship is more than an informant or a stimulus, more even than an inspiration. The teacher is the master to whom loyalty is due, and the loyalty is due both to his doctrine and to his person. The teacher is concerned with the pupil and his growth, but the growth must be in the direction to which the master has dedicated his scholarship and life. In quarrels with other masters the disciples are expected to demonstrate their loyalty or, at least, to refrain from disloyalty. In such a teacher-pupil relationship the character of the teacher and what he teaches are inseparable. The assumption that the skill of the Rhetorician could be regarded apart from the character of both the teacher and the student was precisely what the Socratic method denied.

For Socrates, education and healing were closely related. Like the body, the soul when healthy had its order and form.

It had its proper excellences (virtues) as did the body. To teach was to build in the pupil a system of value priorities and preferences that defined the healthy soul, and not just any order would do. As expounded in the *Republic*, the order of the virtues within the healthy soul was this: reason whose strength constituted the virtue of wisdom was to be the ruler and to dominate in all choice. Appetite or desire for gratification of all sorts was to be subordinated to the judgments of reason, and when this judgment was accepted *willingly*, the person was exercising the virtue of temperance. Courage, or the virtue of maintaining a proper attitude toward danger, meant for Socrates the habitual summoning of emotional resources in favor of the demands of reason and for condemning oneself when behaving contrary to reason. When a human soul functioned in this way, it was a just soul and when, analogously, the various elements within a state were related to each other as reason, appetite, and courage were in the individual, it could be called a just state. This harmony in individual and state was the result of self-discipline. This was produced by a kind of conditioning (training), on the one hand, and by attaining the understanding that intellectually justified the conditioning, on the other. Because the training was to be imposed on the young, the intellectual justification was important, for if there were no standard of right and wrong of which the educator could be certain, then his moral right to impose preferences on the young was put in grave jeopardy.

Socratic Conversation

Everything in the educational scheme depended on the existence of absolute models of the virtues that could be discerned by human beings. Socrates reasoned that inasmuch as absolutes of any kind (ideal forms) could not be found in the world of space and time, then if known at all, they were not learned, but innate. As to why we did not know these from birth, Socrates conjectured that they were forgotten each time the soul was reincarnated in a different body. Hence teaching did not convey these fundamental notions to their learner; it merely prodded him into reminiscing or remembering what he already knew in a previous life but had forgotten.

To illustrate this point, Socrates in the *Meno*, (82a–86b) undertakes to teach a slave boy the proof of the Pythagorean theorem, namely, that the square on the hypotenuse of a right triangle is equal to the sum of the squares on the sides. To begin with, it is determined that the slave boy speaks Greek, knows what a square is like, that it has four equal sides, and that the lines bisecting the sides of the square are equal. He also can count.

The problem is posed: If the given square has a side equal to two feet, what will be the length of the side of a square twice as large?

The boy answers that it will be four feet. Socrates now draws a square presumably of this form:

and asks the boy what would happen to it if he doubled the side. The figure now looks like this:

By counting the squares the boy sees that doubling the side of a square forms a space not twice as large but four times as large.

Socrates begins again. What length of side would give a square containing eight square feet if a two-foot square gives you four square feet? The boy infers that it will be something between two and four feet and guesses at three, but he admits that he doesn't know how to deal with the problem. He has received the shock and is now ready to begin to learn. Socrates begins again drawing the figure:

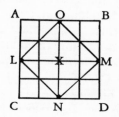

The figure is four times the original one. He draws the diagonals OL, OM, MN, and LN. He asks whether OLNM is a square? Does it have four equal sides? How much space (area) is in this new square?

BOY: I do not understand.

SOC.: Has not each interior line (diagonal) cut off half of the four spaces?

BOY: Yes.

SOC.: How many half-spaces are there in this division [OLNM]?

BOY: Four.

SOC.: How many in this? [OXL]

BOY: Two.

SOC.: And four is how many times two?

BOY: Twice.

SOC.: And this space [OLNM] is of how many feet?

BOY: Of eight feet.

SOC.: And from what line do you get this figure?

BOY: From this. [OL]

SOC.: From the line the learned call the diagonal? Are you prepared to affirm that the double space is the square of the diagonal?

BOY: Certainly, Socrates.

Several points might be noted about this demonstration lesson. A small one is that current interest in teaching mathematics by discovery (Craig, 1956; Haselrud & Meyers, 1958; Hendrix, 1947) is itself a rediscovery. Second, Socrates picked for his demonstration precisely the kind of learning task—a set of deductive relations—that best illustrates the independence of certain conceptual operations from their sources in experience. (Suppose one is told the meaning of "north of," what experience would be needed to conclude that A is north of C, if A is north of B, and B is north of C? This is what is meant by "independence" of experience.) Because the slave boy had not learned the proof from anyone yet understood it, Socrates concluded that the boy had been in possession of the criteria of deductive proof all along and had only to be reminded of them. Third, and perhaps most important, Socrates had hit on the touchy problem of how to teach a deductive system of relations, obviously not by rote memorization, not by imitating a model, and not by learning precepts and rules.

The "moment of truth" in this type of learning comes when the learner grasps the nature of the fundamental mathematical relations involved in the proof and "sees" that so-and-so does not merely happen to be the case, but *must* be the case. The insight having occurred, the learner is ready to go on to mastery, i.e., to supplement understandings with the skills of proof and computation. As to what causes the insight, Socrates had his theory of innate ideas and reminiscence, a theory that to many is not convincing. But is there a convincing theory?

The use of the dialectical conversation or exploration is illustrated in another area by the exchange between Thrasymachus and Socrates in the *Republic* (341–342). Thrasymachus had just argued that a ruler qua ruler makes no mistakes as to what is best for himself, that is, as to where his own interest lies. If the ruler is stronger than the ruled, and if it is right to obey the ruler, then right means whatever is in the interest of the stronger.

To attack this "might is right" doctrine, Socrates gets Thrasymachus to admit that in the case of the physician or ship captain the interest or objective of the craftsmen is not to make money or to serve themselves, but rather to serve their clients.

They agree also that the craft or art is superior to and stronger than the people it serves (i.e., with respect to the skill involved). In serving the clients, the craft or art therefore serves the interests of the weaker rather than the stronger.

If it is objected that this is quibbling over a term, as Thrasymachus did violently object, then Socrates could and did remind him that earlier in the dialogue Thrasymachus had insisted on dealing with the term "ruler" in its strict meaning in order to prove that a ruler could not be mistaken as to what was in his own interest.

In this selection a definition is tested by applying it to cases where it presumably should apply. The test having disconfirmed the definition, a search had to be made for a more adequate definition. A progressive clarification of terms ensues which, according to Plato, can occur only in the dialectical conversation, hence his distrust of the textbook, the written word. Conceptual clarity is achieved by an active search on the part of both learner and teacher for a definition that will stand the dialectical test.

The search, of course, makes no sense unless one believes that there are real definitions of terms and not merely nominal and conventional ones.[2] All of Plato's metaphysics and epistemology were directed toward proving that by careful abstraction and logical analysis the mind could apprehend the essences or the natures of things, and that these universals had a being independent of the particular minds that happened to entertain them and of the objects that exemplified them. With these con-

---

[2] A real definition sets forth those properties that presumably identify the distinctive character of the thing being defined, e.g., defining man as a rational, laughing, biped or a circle as a plane figure all of whose points are equidistant from a point called the center. A conventional definition, on the contrary, stresses those characteristics that serve our purposes of classification. Thus, a cabbage could be defined conventionally by a cook as a vegetable used in the making of cole slaw, by a grocer as a starchy vegetable available throughout the winter months, and by the maker of pesticides as the home of the cabbage worm. Real definitions, if there are any, would give us knowledge about the world; conventional ones inform us about the purposes of men, but not necessarily about the objects being defined.

siderations in mind, an examination of the phases of teaching method that Plato added to Socrates' exhortation and dialectical exploration is in order.

Discipline and Mathematics

How does one teach the learner to apprehend the most general and absolute norms and at the same time to introject them, that is, accept them as his own imperatives for thought and conduct?

Two methods were urged by Plato. Today we might call the first a kind of conditioning. By consistent reinforcement of certain behaviors and the punishment of others, the child was to grow up "spontaneously" loving what he ought to love and hating what he ought to hate, i.e., what his elders who had apprehended the absolute norms knew ought to be loved and ought to be hated.

This training was to be carried on not only by the nurse and teacher, but by the whole cultural milieu as well. The music, the fables, the stories of the gods, every facet of social life was to be controlled to keep the reinforcement uniform. So powerful did Plato regard property and family ties in shaping motives and judgment that he proposed to do away with both in his scheme for the training of the guardians. Freed from these distorting influences the soul was to be made as healthy by music (including literature) as the body was to be made healthy by diet and exercise.

After the future ruler had been inducted into adolescence outfitted with sound habits both of body and of soul, he would, if blessed with adequate mentality, enter upon his secondary education. This consisted of arithmetic, geometry, music, and astronomy, all to be studied in their theoretical aspects rather than in their practical applications to industry or war.

In the *Republic* Plato defends this curriculum as training in abstraction. Apart from his belief that the positive, formative principle of the cosmos and of reality in general was measure, that is, mathematical, he was impressed by the circumstance that mathematics was a system of concepts susceptible of precise definition and rigorous development. The ease with which mathematics could leave the concreteness of objects (their particular size, shape, and color) behind pleased him. To mathematics he gave the second highest rank in knowledge, for it still dealt with hypotheses ("if statements" or stipulated meanings) and drew necessary conclusions within the rules and limitations of the system of meanings itself. Beyond these stipulations it could not go.[3] In their theoretical phase, music and astronomy also exhibited mathematical structures and therefore qualified as training in abstraction to supplement arithmetic, geometry, and solid geometry. There is reason to believe that this kind of study was carried on at Plato's Academy.

The highest level of knowledge, however, was reserved for dialectic in which the deductive relations characteristic of mathematics were discovered to obtain among "real" concepts, that is, the scheme of reality itself. If reality were like a mathematical system, and if the basic primitive propositions could be intuited, metaphysics, the study of the nature of being, would acquire the certainty of mathematics. It would no longer have the contingent nature of a system based on hypotheses only. Furthermore, the disclosures of metaphysics would not have to be derived and learned from sense experience, but would, on the contrary, furnish the eternal norms for interpreting such experience.

The notion of levels of knowledge and levels of perfection is set forth in one of Plato's famous metaphors, the figure of the divided line. In the *Republic* (Book VI) the lowest level of experience is represented as living in a world of shadows in which our knowledge wavers fitfully between myth and distorted perception (*eikasia*), a kind of erratic picture thinking which nevertheless is a genuine attempt to cope with reality. At the next higher level, man lives in the world of opinion and more or less warranted belief. His knowledge corresponds at

---

[3] Thus, if anything is a unicorn, it has a horn in the center of its horselike head; if anything is a satyr, one can predict that it will pursue pretty nymphs; and if anything is a perfect circle, its circumference will contain only points equidistant from the center. That no unicorns, satyrs, and perfect circles exist does not prevent us from manipulating these terms according to the meanings we have chosen to assign them.

this level to what sound common sense can provide; it is picture thinking corrected by rudimentary efforts to make the pictures relevant and consistent (*pistis*). These two lower levels, Plato thought of as being in the domain of sensation, imagination, phantasy, association of ideas, trial-and-error experience, and inferences based upon them.

At a higher level, experience takes a radically different turn. Here the mind asks not only what is the case, but also why it is the case, and indeed, why it could not be otherwise. At this level one is asking for a theory about the world in terms of which it follows that our experience must be what it is. And, of course, once we discover that a theory does explain our experience, we can predict what our experience will be, and this is the first step toward control of it. And so we reach the level of science (*dianoia*) where although we have not yet discovered the ultimate nature of things, we have discovered that if we assume certain things about our world, our theories will "work." The final and highest stage of being and knowledge (*noesis*) is reached when our minds through reason take on the forms of reality itself, and certainty takes the place of plausible and rational guesses. We reach *noesis* by dialectic.

After ten years of studying the secondary subjects, students who survived the testing were to study dialectics for five years. Then they would be drafted for 15 years of public service. What then?

> Then, when they are fifty, those who have come safely through and proved the best at all points in action and in study must be brought at last to the goal. They must lift up the eye of the soul to gaze on that which sheds light on all things; and when they have seen the Good itself, take it as a pattern for the right ordering of the state and of the individual, themselves included (*Republic*, vii. 540, Cornford, 1945, p. 261).

Is this merely a poetic flow of language or did Plato mean to say something about the educational process in this paragraph? I believe the latter to be the more plausible alternative. For Plato all training and study were preliminaries to the act

of conversion—a literal turning of the whole individual into a
new perspective. Indeed Plato himself said:

> Hence there may well be an art whose aim would be to
> effect this very thing, the conversion of the soul, in the
> readiest way; not to put the power of sight into the
> soul's eye, which already has it, but to ensure that, in-
> stead of looking in the wrong direction, it is turned the
> way it ought to be (*Republic*, vii. 518, Cornford, 1945,
> p. 232).

What the Good is that the philosopher will then see is never
made explicit by Plato; but one may speculate that it would
have to be a kind of cognition in which the plan of the universe
its scheme of things entire, its axiological (value) structure,
would become discernible and would be discerned as so self-
authenticating, and so necessary, as to be irresistible both to
mind and to heart.

Perhaps that is why Plato believed that the highest education
required not only instruction and training but fellowship as
well—a way of life, as in a Pythagorean society or perhaps the
society of his own Academy—as a condition for achieving the
conversion. The kind of man he envisioned as a product of this
education could hardly develop in the course of ordinary life,
or if he could, it would be with a frequency no greater than
that which produced a Socrates. This insight history tends to
reconfirm. Even today the scholar is not free from a "conflict of
interest" when he has to integrate his scholarly role with the
domestic, economic, and political roles into which ordinary life
casts him. At another level, we resort to the boarding school as
a specially contrived environment for the education of the
young, insulating them from the influences of the milieu to
which their parents take exception.

From Socrates then comes not the beginning, but rather the
high development of the dialogue as a device for clarifying
problems by sharpening definitions and testing logically the relations among them. The Socratic midwifery, as he called his
teaching (*Theaetetus*), also stressed the psychological notion
that the first step in teaching is the incitement of anxiety in the

learner about the state of his knowledge and his being. This puts a heavy burden on the personality of the teacher. Sophists before him had used logical maneuvers to confound and irritate their pupils. But when Socratic performances in the Platonic dialogues are compared with those of the two Sophists in *Euthydemus,* it is clear that Socrates' indirect communication combined artistically, as the others did not, the comic and the tragic, jest and profound seriousness, logic and myth so as to impress upon his pupil the swing between opposites in life and learning. Lesser talents tend to neglect the comic and thus become pedantic, or they omit the tragic and become buffoons.

From Plato, more than from Socrates, came the suggestion that human perfection might be accelerated by mathematical studies. To understand this, one need only to remember that for Plato, order, proportion, and harmony were as much the signs of perfection as chaos and formlessness were of evil. Mathematical order, therefore, was an ideal that human thought and life should strive to approximate. The heavens and the planets, the seasons of the year, the rhythms of life, of gods and men, it seemed to him, conformed to some formula which, if one were wise enough and godlike enough, could be discerned at the heart of the universe. It would be as revealing of the nature of life of man as of the heavens.

Although Plato's views about mathematics may have been mystical and far-fetched, the developments of modern science bear out the spirit of his speculations, if not the details of his arithmetic. The ideal of description in modern science is the mathematical expression. Until he can reduce his data to such form, the investigator feels that he has not yet penetrated to the ultimate truth of his field of inquiry; when he has expressed them mathematically, he feels there is not much further for him to go. Nevertheless, one should not confuse Plato's respect for mathematics as an educational tool with our respect for mathematics as a theoretical tool. For Plato the study of mathematics was to shape the soul, just as music and literature shape the soul. Harmonious music makes the soul harmonious; mathematical studies make the soul orderly, its thinking clean and precise, and its action just. No such claims are made for the teaching of mathematics today.

Socrates and the Teaching Machine

The current interest in teaching machines points up an important difference in how the art of teaching was viewed by Socrates and Plato, on the one hand, and the Rhetoricians on the other. The Rhetoricians regarded teaching pretty much as systematized imitation. By analyzing procedures in great detail and listing numerous alternatives within each class of operations, it was possible to program the "teaching machine" in clearly definable steps for presenting the task, correcting the trial response, and evaluating the test response.

It is quite a different matter with a Socratic dialogue or the Platonic dialectic. The transaction between teacher and pupil and between both of them and a transcendent ideal requires at least two persons; a machine and a person won't do. The outcome of the teaching is not merely a right response but a response plus an attitude with a complex aura of feeling, an attitude, however, which is not formed once for all. Perhaps it is this aspect of teaching that restrains many schoolmen from an enthusiastic welcoming of the teaching machine. If teaching is a mechanical process, it probably would be more efficient for an electronic machine to do it than a human one, and reluctance with respect to its use would be hard to understand and even harder to defend. If it is to be justified, it is on the grounds that the role of the teacher *as a person* in the teaching transaction is more crucial than the advocates of the machine make it out to be (Broudy, 1963).

It is somewhat puzzling to have programed instruction and teaching machine enthusiasts claim Socrates as their pedagogical patron saint. But perhaps the programers have been too much influenced by the mathematical episode in the *Meno* discussed earlier in the chapter. Although Plato in that dialogue chose an illustration that lent itself to step-by-step programing, its purpose was to illustrate the doctrine of reminiscence, and in any event, Socrates was not noted for his teaching of mathematics.

The reinforcement schedule of the programed text is more like that of the rhetorical exercises than that of the prodding that incited Socrates' pupils to doubt and self-examination. Finally, the Socratic methodology aimed at a new way of thinking and feeling rather than at the mastery of any specific body of content.

That the teacher plays a therapeutic role, a role in group dynamics, a role as father or authority figure—these possibilities have been explored and sometimes deplored. Is there any other role for the teacher? In addition to serving *in loco parentis* and as a substitute psychoanalyst, does he also serve as an image of a value system that, *aesthetically* apprehended, conveys to the student certain models that invite imitation? What sort of clothes, language, voice quality, amusements, and life style in general would make up such a composite image? What value scheme do teachers exemplify as value models? And what value schema are teachers perceived by their pupils as exemplifying? Or do they perceive their teachers as the moving pictures and television have pictured them?

Chapter IV

TEACHING COURTLY BARBARIANS:
ALCUIN

In the century before the reign of Charles I, king of the Franks (Charlemagne), while Western Europe was in a period of cultural decline, learning and education were kept alive in Ireland and the Anglo-Saxon church. They produced Bede (673–735); Egbert, who became archbishop of York in 732 and founded the Cathedral school there; Aelbert, the master of the school under Egbert and later archbishop himself; and Alcuin, who was trained in the Cathedral school and later became its master.

It fell upon Alcuin, born about 735 in northeast England in or near York, to play a singular role in the revival of learning on the continent where nearly four centuries of confusion and barbarian inroads had almost destroyed the schools. A direct line can be traced from Bede, the Cathedral school at York, and Alcuin to the Carolingian revival upon which the culture of the Middle Ages was ultimately to rest. Through the work of scholars associated with these men and institutions, access was obtained to many of the writings current in Roman imperial times—the Latin Vulgate Bible, the works of the Latin Fathers, the treatises of the fourth-century grammarians, the encyclopaedic writings of Cassiodorus and Isidore, the main body of Christian poetry, as well as certain works of Cicero, Virgil, Lucan, and others.

Alcuin's influence as a teacher and stimulant to the intellectual life of his times was especially great because of his obvious talents, but also because he directed schools at York as well as at Tours and Aachen in Gaul. Alcuin held the office of Scholasticus in the Cathedral school at York when he was invited by Charlemagne to assume charge of the Palace school at Aachen.

When he arrived in 782 with his three assistants, he found a situation very different from the one he had known at York.

Nowhere had the decay in Church and State been more pervasive than in Gaul under the latest Merovingian rulers. Differences of race, customs, institutions, and language existed in the several parts of Charles's realm, but all its inhabitants professed a common creed, and the all-embracing Church could serve as the instrument to instruct all the people. From the beginning of his reign, Charles endeavored to raise the cultural level of his subjects, and, as conquest expanded his domain, his zeal increased for spreading education and improving the intellectual life of his people. Because there were no institutions save the clergy and the monasteries that could effect such a plan, the first task was to reform church discipline and improve the educational preparation of the clergy. These tasks were assigned to Alcuin.

The Palace School

The main purpose of the Palace school of the Frankish kings prior to the time of Charles was to train court attendants in proper manners, but the boundless energy and intellectual curiosity of Charles, coupled with his sense of mission in spreading religion and knowledge throughout his kingdom, changed all that. He believed wholeheartedly that he was anointed of God to rule and to promote His earthly kingdom. The latter mission required a clergy able to read and understand the Bible and the writings of the Church Fathers. When he assumed power, only a few priests and scholars were competent in Latin and fewer still in Greek. Under such conditions the purity of the traditional Church was in mortal danger. In addition, because of his own fascination for learning, Charles assumed that knowledge was as necessary for everyone as he felt it was for himself. He brought Alcuin from the center of learning at York to educate himself, his family and court, and through the clergy, the whole. of his realm to insure that the threat of pagan gods might be banished from the kingdom.

Charles expressed his view of the need for education in the following manner in a message to Baugulf, Abbot of Fulda:

> Even as the monastic rule directs purity of conduct, so practice in teaching and learning directs and orders the composition of words, to the end that those who strive to please God by right living may not omit to please Him also by right speaking. . . . We have observed in very many of the aforesaid writings of the same persons right sentiments and uncouth language, because that which pious devotion faithfully dictated inwardly, outwardly, owing to neglect of learning, the untutored tongue could not express without faultiness. Whence it came that we began to fear lest, as skill in writing was less, wisdom to understand the Sacred Scriptures might be far less than it ought rightly to be. And we all know that, though verbal errors are dangerous, errors in interpretation are far more dangerous. Wherefore we exhort you not only not to neglect the study of letters but even with the most humble God-approved earnestness to vie in learning, so that you may prevail more easily and rightly in penetrating the mysteries of sacred literature (Laistner, 1957, pp. 196–197).

The Anglo-Saxon scholar was well suited to this task, for not only was Alcuin an excellent teacher, but he was wholly devoted to the Church and to uplifting the moral life of all men.

Alcuin and his fellow teachers were called upon to work with an odd collection of students at the Palace school. At times all members of the royal family, including Charles and his queen, might be present, together with uncles or aunts or cousins, students, or any visitor who chanced to be at court. It was difficult to distinguish the court life from the operation of the school, because the personnel of court and school were almost identical, and discussion continued beyond formal class sessions. The physical maturity and social status of most of the students, together with the heterogeneous nature of the classes, was undoubtedly responsible for the rather relaxed atmosphere that prevailed in the classroom. The gatherings of monarch, nobility, and apprentice scholars were quite informal, and the continuing members of the inner circle were given pet names taken from Biblical literature of classical antiquity. Charles himself was called David; Alcuin, Flaccus; Einhard, Beseleel, and so forth. These names were used when verses or prose passages on current topics of discussion were exchanged among the group. Alcuin, the acknowledged intellectual leader of this intimate group, viewed each member with great affection and served as counselor and friend.

On serious occasions, antiquarian or dogmatic questions might come up for discussion; at other times, a lighter tone prevailed. Riddles, poems, and witty exchanges provided relief from serious study and contributed to the stimulating atmosphere of the school. Alcuin taxed the group with riddles such as these:

> 89. I saw the dead give birth to the living, and the alive consumed unto death by the living's wrath.
> Pepin ... . answers: "Why, the cooks know the answer to that! It is Fire, born from the friction to dead trees."
> 97. There were three men. One was never born and died once, the second was born once and never died; the third was born once and died twice.
> The answer is: Adam, Elias, Lazarus (Duckett, 1951, pp. 115–116).

In the same vein is a short piece which has come down to us under Alcuin's name, although it is not certain that he wrote it. In any case, it represents one aspect of the teaching common at the time. It is called *Problems for sharpening the Wits of Youth,* and contains 53 puzzles which are solved with very crude methods of calculation used in that period.

> 37. Six labourers were hired to build a house; five of these were experienced, one was a lad, an apprentice. The five men were to divide between them as payment 25 pence a day, less the payment to be made the apprentice, which was to be half an experienced worker's daily wage. How much did each receive a day?
> ... [The answer]: Take 22 pence; give 4 to each man, and the half of this, 2, to the boy. Three pence remain. Divide each penny into 11 parts, making 33 in

all; give 6 of these to each man, making 30, and 3, the correct amount, will be left for the boy.

42. A ladder has 100 steps. On the first sits one pigeon, on the second two, on the third three, and so on up to the hundredth. How many pigeons in all?

. . . arithmetical progression [was] unknown as such to Alcuin. But he calculates:

On step one and step 99 combined sit 100 pigeons, similarly on step 2 and step 98, and so on. Step 50 and step 100 have no pairs.

So his answer is: $49 \times 100 + 50 + 100 = 5050$ pigeons (Duckett, 1951, pp. 116–117)

It is obvious that Alcuin, accustomed to instructing relatively well-prepared boys in the strict atmosphere of the school at York, made many adjustments in order to teach the mature and influential but largely uncultured court members. Theodulf, a resident of the court, described the group in colorful but rather sarcastic terms:

. . . How can the swans be heard to sing when the crows make so much noise? Here the magpie sits at the feast, conceited because he imitates human talk; there the parrot is chattering, ruining Angilbert's verse. One would-be poet struts like a peacock, but only his shrill voice is true to character; another calls the cuckoo's note, or tells of rain, like Virgil's knavish raven, or screeches like the owl that threatens the night (Duckett, 1951, pp. 105–106).

One can well imagine the difficulties that might arise as Alcuin or his assistants pointed out errors in a simple Latin sentence written by a favorite military lieutenant of Charles's or the wife of an influential noble. The adult "parrot" or "peacock" could hardly be dealt with by the schoolmaster in the same manner as a young pupil. Both parties to the situation at Aachen are to be commended—Alcuin for being able to accomplish his task with remarkable success and to maintain the affection of his adult pupils; the pupils for their perseverance in trying to learn what for them was a difficult foreign language. For both, the compelling force of religion was undoubtedly crucial, although the authority of Charles was no mean factor in the situation. It behooved the prudent organization man of that day to share the enthusiasm of his ruler.

Instruction was especially difficult in the Palace school, because the earlier educational system of Gaul had completely disappeared. Even the training of the clergy had been seriously impaired by the widespread illiteracy. In moving from York, Alcuin had truly left a center of learning for an intellectual desert. His writings refer to his "daily fights" with the rusticity of his adult pupils. That schooling should assume an elementary form was inevitable. The key to the literary treasures of the past was a knowledge of Latin, a language that had all but died out in Gaul. In the monastic schools of the period the earlier compromise arrived at by the Latin Fathers was still maintained, their main object being not so much the creation of Latin *litterateurs* as the training of ecclesiastics for the performance of their duties. To that end the study of secular literature, and more particularly its grammatical principles, was considered necessary, although Bede's admonition "to pluck the flowers and fruits, but beware of the lurking snakes" was closely followed. Thus grammar, which at Rome had prepared the way for rhetoric, became the recognized preliminary to the understanding of the Scriptures.

Literacy for Adults

Many of the Palace students, their roles in the economic and social life of the country already firmly established, had neither desire nor opportunity to become scholars, but were satisfied to acquire the most elementary attribute of culture at the time, some proficiency in Latin. Alcuin's task was not one of stimulating them to move into new frontiers of learning but rather to school them so thoroughly in Latin that they could read and write correctly and not distort the wisdom contained in the Scriptures or the classics.

The overwhelming emphasis on correct phrasing, grammatical construction, and spelling lea quite naturally to drill and repetitive exercises, quite as if the questions and answers were programed for a modern teaching machine. Meaning, particularly of the Scriptures, was handled in a similar fashion, the interpretation of key phrases and passages being supplied for the student to commit to memory. Originality and creativity were little honored in language study. Truth and falsity, correctness and error, were clearly defined, at least in the things that would engage ordinary men. This seemed appropriate when dealing with the uncultured Franks. Alcuin did not see himself as an originator but as a preserver and conveyor. Nothing could be, should be, devised or added to the words of authority, save exhortation to their study. He strove to substantiate every belief or claim to truth by direct citation of a Church Father or Scripture.

At the beginning of Alcuin's *De grammatica* a teacher is asked by his students to explain the various stages of the ladder that leads up to philosophy. As fire lies buried in the flint, so deep within the human mind lies the desire for wisdom. But, as the flint must be struck, so must the mind of the learner be stimulated by a teacher's working on it. True wisdom is based on the seven liberal arts, but in the book Alcuin deals only with grammar. He imagines a discussion between himself as a teacher and two of his students who ask him questions. The dialogue deals exclusively and methodically with the parts of speech. The material is presented in an elementary fashion adapted to "those who had but lately rushed upon the thorny thickets of grammatical density." The two students, a Saxon and a Frank, having but recently begun the study of grammatical subtleties, have decided to question each other in order to aid their memory in mastering the rules of grammar. It is agreed that all difficult questions will be referred to the master. The latter begins their "disputation" by starting them off in a discussion of "littera."

FRANK: Why, Saxon, is it called "littera"?
SAXON: Because the letter prepares the path for the reader.
FRANK: Give me then a definition of "littera."
SAXON: It is the smallest part of articulate voice.
BOTH: Master, is there another definition?
MASTER: There is, but of similar import. The letter is indivisible, because we divide the sentences

	into parts, and the parts into syllables and the latter into letters, which are thus indivisible.
BOTH:	Why do you call letters, elements?
MASTER:	Because as the members fitly joined together make the body, so the letters make speech.
FRANK:	State, my fellow pupil, the kinds of letters.
SAXON:	They are vowels and consonants, which may be further sub-divided into semi-vowels and mutes . . . (Page, 1909, pp. 79–80).

The parts of speech are treated in the same way, with definitions and irregularities stressed throughout. The verb is treated extensively, and in the course of the dialogue the Saxon gives an appalling list of irregularities in mode and tense. So formidable is it that the Saxon himself is dismayed and discouraged. "Lo, Frank," he states, "what a burden you have laid upon me! What a thorny path you have led me into! Let us have a moment's breathing space, I pray you." "So be it," replied the Frank: "As Virgil saith, 'I shall crush you with this weight.' Yet fear not 'Labor vincit omnia.'" "'Tis so," agrees the Saxon wearily, "let us continue" (Page, 1909, p. 81).

De orthographia, which lacks direct indication of teaching method, is a list of words, arranged in alphabetical order, as was Bede's work on the same subject, and intended to teach the proper forms, declensions, and usages according to traditional custom. A concession to the widespread illiteracy, its main objects were to secure accurate spelling and the proper use of Latin words while at the same time attempting to free Latin from its many barbarisms.

Further examples of Alcuin's method are provided in the *Disputatio* and *De rhetorica*.

A Class Discussion

In the *Disputatio* the young Pippin asks the questions, Albinus (Alcuin) replies.

Pippinus:	What is a letter?
Albinus:	The guardian of history.
P.:	What is a word?
A.:	The mind's betrayer.

P.:	What creates the word?
A.:	The tongue.
P.:	What is the tongue?
A.:	Something which whips the air.
P.:	What is the air?
A.:	The protection of life.
P.:	What is life?
A.:	The joy of the blessed, the sorrow of sinners, the expectation of death.
P.:	What is death?
A.:	An unavoidable occurrence, an uncertain journey, the tears of living, the confirmation of the testament, the thief of man.
P.:	What is man?
A.:	The slave of death, a passing wayfarer, the guest of a place.
P.:	To what is man like?
A.:	A fruit.
P.:	How is man situated?
A.:	Like a lamp in the wind.
P.:	Where is he situated?
A.:	Within six walls.
P.:	Which?
A.:	Above, below, before, behind, right and left (Laistner, 1957, p. 199).

The answers throughout betray that fondness for verbal enigmas which was to be so characteristic of the more educated men in the Middle Ages. While the dull student undoubtedly viewed these answers as so many sentences to be committed to memory, the bright were stimulated to improve upon them, to develop more profound or abstruse answers, and to wonder over the full import of the response.

In the following passage from the *De rhetorica* the speakers are Alcuin and Charles. In the earlier part of the dialogue Alcuin asks the questions; in the portion cited, however, it is his turn to take over the exposition.

Carolus:	Expound the nature of justice.
Albinus:	Justice is a state of mind which assigns to each thing its proper worth. In it the cult of the divine, the rights of mankind, and the equitable state of the whole of life are preserved.

C.:   Unfold its parts also.

A.:   Justice proceeds in part from natural right, partly from customary use.

C.:   How does it proceed from natural right?

A.:   Because a certain natural force engenders its parts, namely, religion, dutifulness (*pietas*), gratitude, requital (*vindicatio*), observance, truth.

C.:   Explain each of these more clearly.

A.:   Religion is that which pays heed and rites to a nature, which men call divine, of some superior Being. Dutifulness is that through which one bestows on blood relatives and well-wishers of one's country service and loving homage. Gratitude is the quality in which is contained the remembrance of friendships and good offices of one's neighbors and the wish to reward him. Requital is that by which right and injury and everything that meets us is by defence or retribution advanced. Observance is the quality with which we deem those who are our superiors in worth worthy of a certain degree of veneration and honour. Truth is that through which what is, what has been, and what will be, is denoted.

C.:   How is justice which proceeds from customary use maintained?

A.:   By contract, by equity, by judgement, and by law.

C.:   I would fain hear more about these also.

A.:   Contract is an agreement between persons. Equity is that which is fair to all. Judgement is what is established by the opinions of a prominent man or of several. Law is right written down for all the people (stating) of what it is their duty to beware and what to hold fast (Laistner, 1957, pp. 200–201).

The substantive content of these books was borrowed from earlier sources. The form illustrates the type of conversation which master and pupil might hold, and it constituted the primary teaching procedure. Many of these books were used as texts long after Alcuin's death.

The limitations of Alcuin's works are obvious, particularly with respect to the narrow conception of grammar they convey.

Ignoring the critical study of literature, grammar becomes a technical and mechanical exercise largely devoid of literary interest. It lost the larger meaning that Quintilian had given it. There was, for example, no place in it for the interpretation of poetry. Nor did it include the philosophical inquiry bound up with the work of Priscian. Its aim was purely utilitarian; a means of adapting ancient culture to religious education. Nevertheless, it must be conceded that Alcuin's subject matter and methodology were well suited to his students, if one keeps in mind contemporary conditions, the state of learning, and the intellectual darkness that prevailed in the land. His aim was limited to the development of reading and writing skills with moral virtue as a by-product. His effort was limited by ecclesiastical and political needs. Yet it represented the earliest direct contact of the Middle Ages with the teaching of ancient Rome. It acquainted men with the classical conceptions of plainness and clearness of expression, skill in the choice and handling of words, the importance of constant practice, and the observance of *decorum*.

Judged by his writings on education, Alcuin developed no original ideas but was content to compile dull compendiums of the works of authorities for use in exercise and drill of backward pupils. He made, however, a most significant mark as a teacher. The list of those who were his pupils at the Palace school, and after 796, at Tours, contained many famous names including Einhard, Grimald, and Rhabanus Maurus. As a master he was spoken of in terms of affectionate and grateful admiration. On many occasions Alcuin wrote to former students as a father might write to a son concerning his moral and intellectual life. The close personal bond that developed between master and student was an integral part of his methodology. The informality of procedure in the Palace school, although annoying to him at times, was compatible with his love of people and intellectual discussion.

The unique challenge facing Alcuin as a teacher was that of educating adults in a relatively barbaric setting. He had to teach elementary knowledge to students who were mature of body and mind but lacked formal educational experience. Years ago our society faced a somewhat similar instructional situation with the waves of immigrants who had a wide range of ability and previous education but needed to learn a new language and way of life. The problem of adult elementary education in our day has taken on a different character, for it involves a portion of the native population that is culturally as well as economically deprived. While the circumstances are hardly analogous, it is interesting to speculate on the critical factors that may have accounted for Alcuin's success in adult education and which might be put to use today.

Although he voiced mild discontent on occasion, Alcuin accepted the students for what they were and went on from where they were. The Palace school left much to be desired if judged by the best schools of the day in England and Ireland. One wonders, had communications been better, if Alcuin would have felt as free to meet his pupils on their own ground. Would he have lost face and status with his old colleagues at York? Alcuin's compelling sense of mission in bringing learning to the Franks and his technique of leavening dull drill with riddles and other challenges to the student's creativity should not be overlooked. While the students may have recognized the elementary character of much of what they did, Alcuin gave them the sense of being intellectually respectable by encouraging them to match wits with him in composing poetry, answering riddles, and solving puzzles.

Perhaps more significant than any of these devices was the desire common to all to draw nearer to Divine truth through a better understanding of religious literature. This supreme value, so compelling to every individual at the time, overshadowed the personal wishes and difficulties of both teacher and pupils. If tedious hours spent in memorizing verb forms would further their goal, then the effort was well worth it. Thus, although the instruction was directed toward the symbolic skills and for the prospective clergyman furnished a species of vocational training, it was as much a training for virtue as for success. The road to virtue being religion and the road to religion being the knowledge of religious language, the educational enterprise acquired a character and tone that made it more than remedial literacy or a royal hobby.

Chapter V

SCHOLASTICISM AS A METHOD OF TEACHING: ABELARD

Alcuin faced the problem of keeping the rudiments of learning alive in an adult society that had lost touch with the classical literatures of the Greeks and the Romans, and in which the arts of rhetoric were of little use as a means of gaining power and prestige. In the next few centuries, however, monastery schools and schools attached to the great cathedrals gave instruction in the seven liberal arts and in the writings of the Church. Here and there a thinker such as John the Scot, influenced by Greek thought, began to use formal logic to examine the relationship between the authority of the Church and the demands of human reason. In many of the cathedral schools, courses in theology were offered. It was almost inevitable that the dialectical or debating aspects of oratory and rhetoric would be used in discussing the problems of theology so vital in an age when the Church was so important a social institution. Just as a new revival of learning was about to take place and just before the university was to blossom in Europe as the educational institution par excellence, we encounter a brilliant teacher who served as a kind of bridge between the cathedral school and the university.

Peter Abelard (1079–1142) deserves a place in the history of teaching for a number of reasons. First of all, he was a teacher and a teacher of teachers. All of his glory and most of his professional difficulties were related to his teaching activity.

Second, his teaching employed a method of structuring and presenting materials that set the style for the age of Scholastic education.

Third, his personality made him one of those teachers who needs no special means of motivating his classes. He drew throngs wherever he taught. There seems to be little doubt that he was a man "of combative disposition and unsparing of his adversaries," not excluding his own master, William of Champeaux (1070–1120) and the formidable St. Bernard of Clairvaux, who successfully accused him of heresy. According to one commentator, Abelard was difficult to get along with and left both the Abbey of St. Denis and that of St. Gildas because he was "unable to live in peace with the other monks, . . ." (Copleston, 1962, I, 170).

Fourth, we have in Abelard a prime example of how current controversies dominate the content and methods of teaching.

Finally, he is an exemplar of higher education, if by higher we mean training in use and evaluation of cognitive materials rather than in the acquisition of basic skills and concepts.

Abelard's great fame came after he was 37 years of age. He attracted students from all parts of the Western world to Paris, where he taught at Notre Dame and the collegiate church of St. Genevieve. After *l'affaire Héloise* he was in more or less continuous warfare with his enemies. Inasmuch as they were very powerful, he was forever taking refuge in this or that monastery, but despite his disgrace and humiliation, Abelard had but to get behind a lectern and students flocked to hear him, and among them must have been young men of high caliber, because it is reported that 20 of his pupils became cardinals and 50 others became bishops (Rashdall, 1936, I, 58–59).

Controversy and Motivation

It is commonly said that the medieval ages were agog over the problem of universals, and this is likely to be shrugged off as an historical aberration much on the order of the question of how many angels could stand on the head of a pin. That we find it difficult to understand the excitement of the medieval ages over the ontological status of universals or the spatial characteristics of angels is not surprising. However, in an age when sin, redemption, salvation, faith, and God were important to all people, the conceptual apparatus lying at their foundations was as absorbing to intellectuals as mathematics, physics, atomic warfare, and space exploration are to intellectuals now.

Both to men of simple faith and to men of faith who were highly sophisticated in secular learning, as many of Abelard's contemporaries were, the Trinity, Creation, Redemption, and Resurrection were to be taken as part of the Christian revelation vouchsafed to those with a faith in this revelation.

Yet to many intellectuals of the twelfth and thirteenth centuries, increasingly familiar with the teachings of Plato and Aristotle in logic, metaphysics, and the other branches of philosophy, the absolute distinction between a faith and reason was hard to maintain. The Christian theology had to be reconciled with philosophy. It so happened that the crux of many of these problems was located in the ontological status of universals, i.e., whether properties shared by all members of a class, e.g., humanity, had independent being, or were names of classes, or constructs of the human mind. The problem is as old as philosophy itself, but such questions as whether the persons of the Trinity were one or three; whether man's humanity was one or subdivided among all living men (and perhaps dead ones, too) made the problem a matter of life and religious faith as well as an intellectual puzzle.

The tension between the demands of intellectual and doctrinal adequacy paved the way for Scholasticism, the application of philosophical concepts and method to theology that was to become the method of the universities in the thirteenth century. It is as precursor of Scholasticism that Abelard is so important in pedagogy (Harnack, 1896–1899, VI, 42), although this characterization has occasionally been challenged (Sikes, 1932).

The very presumption that an application of rational, secular philosophy to theology could be made at all shocked some of Abelard's famous contemporaries and earned him their sincere enmity. Bernard of Clairveaux was his archenemy and he was not alone, but the tide of the times was with Abelard.

The validating sources of Christian doctrine (or, with appropriate variations, of Judaic or Islamic doctrine, for that matter) were the Scriptures, the writings of the Church Fathers, and official doctrines promulgated by the Church. None of these could be regarded as false—even hypothetically—because they were presumed to be directly or indirectly inspired by God.

On the other hand, the validating sources of human thought were the principles of logic and the results of philosophy that were authenticated by logical argument. Thus, for example, *ex nihilo nihil fit* (out of nothing, nothing comes) is an indispensable principle both to logic and to rational thought in general. If the principle is accepted however, what is one to do with the Christian doctrine of Divine creation? The principles of logic do not take kindly to contradictory statements adduced as evidence for this or that doctrinal position. What was one to do, when, as so often happened, statements from the Scriptures did seem to be saying contradictory things about important dogmas?

Abelard's Dialectic

In *Sic et Non,* Abelard formulated 158 questions about the Trinity, Redemption, and the Sacraments. In one column he placed the "Yes" answers from the authorities; in an opposite column the "No" answers. More accurately, he marshaled the validating citations for the affirmative and negative sides of the question in opposite columns.

How were these "contradictions" to be reconciled?

1. The question having been stated and the incompatible *dicta* lined up, the context of each of them was to be explored. Read in their context, would the *dicta* still be contradictory? What would enable Abelard to establish these contexts? Only some sort of historical scholarship undertaken by himself or by other scholars in the field. Presumably the new type of teacher would have to include such scholarship in his pedagogical arsenal.

2. Next, textual corruptions were to be located and disproven. If the passages cited as evidence had been distorted by copyists, forgers, and other hazards of transmission, they would lose their face evidential value. Hence, textual criticism entailing knowledge of etymology, morphology of grammatical forms, and other elements of linguistic science and history would be

brought into play. Precisely such skills were supposed to be imparted in the earlier grammar schools and in the school of Rhetoric (Quintilian *Institutio*, I, vi).

3. The stage was now set to make a judgment as to the *real* meaning of each of the passages cited, as distinguished from the incidental meaning it conveyed. If one compared a passage with others and got help from authoritative glosses, this judgment need not be arbitrary.

4. Next, one was to make sure that there was no retraction of the cited passages on record.

5. Finally, one was to search out the facts that led up to the enactment of an ordinance or the making of a decision by the Church or some Council of the Church. These data would help fix the inner meanings or intent of the passage, much as we now try to fix the meaning of certain passages in the United States Constitution by inquiring into the circumstances that led to the writing of these passages.

6. If incompatibilities still remained, the rules of the game required one of two conclusions: (a) this was a mystery to be believed, or (b) a theory was needed in the light of which both sides would be correct but only partial views or aspects of the truth. Abelard himself came up with such a formulation in the status of the universals.

Realists of the Platonic type argued that the characteristics that distinguished one species or class of things from all others, e.g., the characteristics that distinguish "dogness" from "catness," must exist prior to and apart from individual cats and dogs. An invariant world of forms (essences, universals) in which the individual things "participated" provided the world of time and space with the stability that permitted it to be (*esse*) and to be known. Aristotle, finding difficulty with Plato's separate world of forms (universals), placed them in the individual things themselves, saying that if things are to be and to be known by their invariant structures, then these structures must be the formal properties of things *in* the world. Rejecting both the extreme realism of Plato and the moderate realism of Aristotle, the Nominalists argued that universals were no more real than names that we attach to characteristics of "dogness" and "catness" after noting the appearance of a sufficient number of these animals.

Abelard argued that universals exist *before* things (Plato) in the mind of God; *in* things as their discernible likenesses (Aristotle); and *after* things as likenesses discerned by the learner or by inquiring minds (Nominalism). Thus, by making a set of epistemological and ontological distinctions, Abelard could, at least to his own satisfaction, solve some of the problems he had raised.

The resemblances of Abelard's procedure to the Socratic dialectic and to the forensic techniques of the Rhetoricians are fairly obvious. DeWulf (1922, p. 163) calls the method "apologetics." Others believe that Abelard adapted the methods of the canon lawyers to the study of theology (Sikes, 1932, p. 85), and still others refer to his method as something between the Socratic dialogue and the modern case study (Moore, 1938, II, 320). Abelard regarded logic as the method whereby arguments could be discovered to defend the truth of Christian doctrines; dialectic was the means by which contradictions among authorities were to be resolved (Sikes, 1932, p. 88).

The Lecture and the Disputation

The core of Scholastic instruction was the lecture. When books were scarce, the lecture was, to a large extent, the reading of a book by the master while the pupils copied down what he said. Depending on his erudition and the nature of the subject, the master might embellish the reading with commentaries and explanations. Or, following Abelard, the lecturer might "determine" or argue a question in theology or philosophy by the reconciliation method described above.

Abelard often had to conduct these disputations with one of his doctrinal enemies in public. Notable occasions, these disputations were responsible for a large part of his popularity. There were, no doubt, many such debates between masters, and what would be more natural than that prospective teachers should try their hand at both a lecture in which they argued a question themselves and a disputation with a real opponent?

This debate—not, strictly speaking, a teaching device—must have done much to establish one's status as a teacher. Dialectical competence became a requisite for all teaching in the higher faculties. Hence the disputation and the *determinatio* also became features of teacher preparation as well as ingredients of the ceremonies leading to advanced degrees, that is, licenses to teach.

The lecture form of university teaching put a premium on commentaries, short tracts, and elaborate treatises (*summae*) that provided the teacher with material for his discourses on important issues. There were also collections of *Questiones* containing transcripts of debates or the arguments to be used in debating certain issues, e.g., Peter Lombard's *Sentences*.

By the time of St. Thomas Aquinas the method of logical demonstration had been perfected. Armed with the mastery of Aristotelian philosophy and the results of theological scholarship, he began with a question, reviewed the authorities, proposed the correct solution, and then systematically refuted all the objections which he thought could be brought against it. In one sense, St. Thomas' method was the culmination of Abelard's subjection of theological questions to rational examination. In another sense, it paved the way for a method of teaching that could dispense with genuine doubt and inquiry and settle for a memorization of St. Thomas' *Summae*. Once an authority of St. Thomas' magnitude gave the answers in a textbook, the temptation to leave out the logical work that went into Thomas' thinking reared its head, and, no doubt, many a master yielded to it. Scholasticism built reason into its dogma. The effect was to make the dogma more rational but also to make a certain type of reasoning dogmatic.

By the end of the thirteenth century, at the University of Paris, the rules and nature of the disputation had been defined. Many students at the medieval universities were really apprentice teachers trying to qualify for membership in the teachers' guild—the guild of masters. They often played at being masters before they were old enough to be admitted to the guild. By 1279, playing at giving lectures and disputing a thesis became obligatory before one could qualify for the Chancellor's license to teach. To protect their own reputations and to make sure their students could hold their own in a public disputation, the masters ruled that a prospective determiner or debater must first hold a disputation with a master and then face examiners appointed by their national group. If successful, the student became a bachelor, a sort of assistant teacher (Moore, 1938, II, 362–364).

Rashdall notes (1936, III, 452) that in the higher faculties of the university one encountered a tendency on the part of the doctors to evade the obligation of teaching without surrendering its emoluments, while the real teaching devolved upon half-trained bachelors; that is, ". . . in medieval times students were more anxious to learn than the teachers were to teach,"—a tendency not without its modern counterpart.

Bachelors gave lectures modeled after the master's and conducted reviews (repetitions). At Bologna a bachelor was required to give a course of lectures or a repetition and to have completed seven or eight years of study for a degree in civil law or six years in study for a degree in canon law. Sometimes to fulfill the lecturing requirement, the student had to bribe students to sit under him. Thus what probably began as an informal playing at teaching turned into a formal requirement for entrance into the teaching profession. Here are excerpts from an imaginary reconstruction of such a debate:

> The assailant having first denied that *An external world exists,* which is of course asserted by the defender, proceeds to prove his case as follows:
>
> No world independent of consciousness exists;
> Now, an external world is a world independent of consciousness;
> Therefore, no external world exists.
>
> DEFENDER: At the major premiss, 'No world independent of consciousness exists,' I take a distinction. No world independent of *all* consciousness? I waive that question. No world independent of *my* consciousness exists? I deny it.—At the minor, 'An external world is a world independent of consciousness.' I counter-distinguish. Of *all* consciousness? I deny

it. Of *my* consciousness? I grant that. By this distinction your argument is out of form and inadmissible.

ASSAILANT: But no external world independent of *my* consciousness exists; therefore, your distinction is worthless.

DEFENDER: I deny that.

ASSAILANT: I prove it. Nothing but a modification of myself exists; Now, a world independent of my consciousness is not a modification of myself; therefore, No world independent of my con-consciousness exists.

DEFENDER: At the major, 'Nothing but the modification of myself exists,' I distinguish. Exists *as my perception?* I admit that. Exists as the cause of my perception? I deny it.—As for the minor, 'A world independent of my consciousness is not a modification of myself,' I grant that. So I distinguish the conclusion: 'No world independent of my consciousness exists': *as my perception?* I grant it. *As the cause* of my perception? I deny that.

ASSAILANT: But my perception and the cause of my perception are identical; therfore, your distinction is worthless.

DEFENDER: I deny that.

ASSAILANT: I prove it. What is perceived by me is the cause of my perception; But my perception is what is perceived by me; therefore, My perception is the same as the cause of my perception.

DEFENDER: 'What is perceived by me is the cause of my perception': here I distinguish. What is perceived by me *as something in myself* is the cause of my perception? That I deny. What is perceived by me *as something outside of myself* is the cause of my perception? I grant it.—As for the minor, 'My perception is what is perceived by me,' I counter-distinguish. Is what is perceived by me *as something outside of myself?* I deny that. By this distinction, your argument is out of form, and inadmissible.

ASSAILANT: But to perceive what is outside of self is absurd; therefore, your distinction is worthless.

DEFENDER: I deny that.

ASSAILANT: I prove it. To have within self what is outside of self is absurd; now to perceive what
is outside of self is to have within self what
is outside of self; therefore, to perceive what
is outside of self is absurd.

DEFENDER: I distinguish your major. To have within self
really what is *really* outside of self is absurd?
That I admit. To have within self *ideally*
what is *really* outside of self is absurd? I
deny it.—I counter-distinguish your minor. To
perceive what is outside of self is to have
within self *really* what is *really* outside of
self? I deny it. Is to have *ideally* within self
what is *really* outside of self? I admit that.
By this distinction your argument is out of
form and inadmissible. (Winterton, 1888, as
quoted in Moore, 1938, II, 361–363).

This somewhat bewildering display of dialectical fencing
represents the extreme formalizing of the Socratic dialogue. It is
far more precise and rigorous than a Socratic dialogue, but it
impresses us as being verbalistic and trivial—a kind of word
chess—a verbal game.

The formalization was achieved first by strict adherence to
the rules and moves of the syllogism, which the disputant knew
and could use as skillfully as the tennis player knows and uses
the rules and strokes of his game. He knew just which moves
were permitted and which ones he could make in order to
invalidate his opponent's argument and to validate his own. In
the second place, the distinctions that each made and used
throughout the disputation were not invented on the spot; they
were as standard as certain gambits in chess. Nevertheless, the
rules and the arguments had to be learned and, one might add,
understood as well. In addition, there had to be long practice
in the use of them in the debating situation.

In later days men passed harsh judgment on medieval disputations as empty verbalistic exercises. Yet if it is kept in mind
that the prospective teacher would one day have to conduct
public disputations and give dialectical lectures, their use in
the university constituted a most practical sort of practice teach-

ing. That the masters continued to hold highly formalized disputations long after interest had shifted to subject matter for which the formal disputation was inappropriate is a more serious but a quite different indictment. Pedagogical lag, however, was not peculiar to Scholasticism. It is an indictment of academicians in every age. Course content and classroom procedure are almost never abreast of the best knowledge of the time. It is only at the topmost level of graduate instruction that the content of teaching and research converge.

As a method of teacher training, the disputation warrants another glance. To what extent is a high school or college teacher required to use dialectical skill in teaching? Much of what we now try to teach involves the rules of thinking games: the rules of deduction and induction, or the rules of evidence in making assertions. This might be called the logic of the subject matter and teaching (Smith, 1960, p. 237). To what extent should prospective teachers be given the kind of practice that corresponds to the disputation? Have the potentialities of formal debating really been exploited in this connection? The oral examination on the doctoral dissertation is the vestigial remnant of the public disputation. This logical sparring is not, however, regarded as practice teaching, although in many instances this is about all the practice in the logic of teaching that a prospective college teacher gets.

Observations

The lecture, the repetition, and the disputation constituted the method of the medieval universities. The lecture developed from the mere reading of scarce textbooks to the summarizations of authorities and commentaries upon them; that is, the lecture became interpretive and critical.

When the commentaries and summaries were themselves put into textbook form, the lecturer had to give new interpretations or explain difficulties, i.e., do something the book did not do. In one sense the textbook makers are in constant pursuit of the lecturer—intent on making him superfluous and often succeeding without the victim's being aware of it.

Later, at the University of Halle (founded in 1694), the lecture was transformed from a commentary on the text to the systematic presentation of a growing field of knowledge by the research workers or advanced students of the field (Brubacher, 1947, p. 181).

The repetition was not a literal duplication of the lecture, but rather an elaboration of topics and questions growing out of it. At Oxford, lectures were supplemented by *resumpciones,* small informal groups in which scholars were examined by the lecturer or some other master or bachelor on the subject of the lecture (Rashdall, 1936, III, 398–399).

The repetition and the *resumpciones* can be viewed as trial runs to check on the way the student had perceived the materials to be learned. It is a truism that the student hears and reads selectively and that he classifies what he hears and reads in terms of his own categories and interests. The teacher never really knows what the student selected until he tests it by a recitation or an examination, and perhaps not even then. Orderliness in textbooks and lucidity in lectures cannot guarantee that the selection by the student will be the one intended by the teacher. The ancients may have erred on the side of overdetermining the student's selection; perhaps this charge could properly be leveled against all traditional schooling. However, the other extreme is not without its dangers. One may venture the suggestion that either extreme is less confusing than the combination of understructured teaching and overstructured testing. To demand on a test that the pupil reproduce the structure of the text when no particular effort has been made to teach that structure is a strange but not uncommon form of pedagogical irrelevance.

Chapter VI

METHODS OF
TEACHING CLASSICS TO GENTLEMEN:
ASCHAM AND THE JESUITS

> Humanistic education, based on the great intellectual inheritance recovered from the ancient world by a relatively small number of Italian scholars, dominated the secondary-school training of the middle and higher classes of society for the next four hundred years (Cubberley, 1920a, p. 263).

The four centuries extended from about 1450 to 1850. Educationally, not the least significant of these recoveries or revivals were Cicero's orations and later a complete copy of Quintilian's *Institutes of Oratory* at St. Gall (Cubberley, 1920a, p. 265). These furnished once more the archetype or master model for Latin style and for a method to teach that style.

Owing to many factors that cannot be discussed here, the ideal of the cultured gentleman—fit for the demands of citizenship, the new world of commerce, the affairs at court diplomatic and otherwise—became the educational image of a life style. The Renaissance focused its energies on the revival of the Greek and Roman ideal of human life, an ideal that has a strange perennial fascination for Western man. It was believed that the literatures of Greece and Rome had everything needed to educate the model man. Battista Guarino put it simply: "I have said that ability to write Latin verse is one of the essential marks of an educated person. I wish now to indicate a second . . . familiarity with the language and literature of Greece" (Cubberley, 1920b, p. 205).

The classic literatures had elegance of style wherewith to

71

make language persuasive, and knowledge to serve as a basis of wisdom in conduct. Milton and Montaigne looked to the classical literatures for useful knowledge and moral wisdom; others were fascinated by its literary elegance, and still others were willing to settle for formal and verbal conformity to the writings of Cicero, hopeful that by some pedagogical alchemy the powers to think, imagine, remember, and judge would flow from the foaming beaker of Latin study.

In time the spirit of the Renaissance permeated the schools. Both spirit and content pervaded such diverse institutions as Johann Sturm's (1507–1589) famous *Gymnasium* in Strasbourg, Calvin's colleges in France and Switzerland, Colet's school at St. Paul, and all the better grammar schools in England. They also pervaded the schools set up by the Jesuits under the influence of Ignatius de Loyola (1491–1556), which will be discussed shortly.

Roger Ascham

. . . nobility governed by learning and wisdom is indeed most like a fair ship, having tide and wind at will, under the rule of a skilful master; when contrary wise a ship carried, yea, with the highest tide and greatest wind, lacking a skilful master, most commonly doth either sink itself upon sands or break itself upon rocks. . . . Therefore, ye great and noblemen's children, if ye will have rightfully that praise and enjoy surely that place which your fathers have and elders had, and left unto you, ye must keep it as they got it, and that is by the only way of virtue, wisdom, and worthiness (Ascham, 1900, pp. 46–47).

With these words Roger Ascham in the middle of the sixteenth century charged the governing class of England with its responsibility to train its young so that they might rule well. While training for service to the Church was not overlooked, it had to make room for the administration of worldly affairs, particularly the exercise of political power. The educational scheme that was ultimately developed to prepare the governing class for their important earthly tasks was intimately connected with the spirit of the Renaissance.

As the ideas and ideals of the Renaissance swept from south to north in Europe during the two centuries preceding Ascham's time, three types of inquiry competed for allegiance among scholars and teachers. The firmly established Scholastic methods of theology, which looked to religious doctrine and Aristotelian philosophy for authority, were challenged, on the one hand, by the inductive methods of science, which placed the locus of authority in Nature, and on the other, by the literary and linguistic methods of Humanism, which looked to the ancient classics for authority. The Humanists won the day, although the victory was only a temporary one.

The prime instruments of human intelligence were considered by the Humanists to be grammar and rhetoric. They viewed the literary accomplishments of reading, writing, and rhetorical composition as the highest achievements of the human mind and as the means by which the intellect might be cultivated to its highest form. The standards of all types of value as well as of literary excellence were to be found in the great masterpieces of Greek and Latin literature.

Correlated with this fundamental notion in the development of a theory of education were the individualism, the worldly interests, and the general optimism of the Renaissance man. The aim of the Humanistic education was to produce a broadly educated person with a well-rounded personality, one who was capable of assuming leadership in Church or State. He was to be at home in the field of classical knowledge and yet be an effective man of action and citizen. He was to possess a wide range of accomplishments in poetry, song, dance, physical prowess, but at the same time he was to be a Christian gentleman with all the social graces. Montaigne was of the opinion that he should also be trained to undertake courtly dissipations with fortitude and decorum.

The curriculum designed to produce such a man leaned heavily on the classical literature of Greece and Rome. The restoration of Greek language and literature to a prominent place in the curriculum revived the ideal of the full man and the idea of a "liberal" education. These were well suited to the demands of the time, at least for the ruling class. Whereas training in Latin during the Middle Ages was a species of vocational training for the clerical professions, Greek was not directly useful but rather a way of training the mind, and more particularly, the mind of a gentleman. Under the influence of the Greek ideal of physical beauty, the human body took on a new dignity, and physical exercise became an honorable activity for the gentleman. In England, for example, Eton acquired a large playing field designed to give physical exercise and training for the "battles of life."

The works of Quintilian and Cicero occupied center stage in the restoration of classical Latin. As a result of the rediscovery of Quintilian, the ancient ideal of the "good man skilled in speaking" was revived. Cicero became the model of Latin style and was to survive as Ciceronism in the schools long after the Renaissance was over.

At its best, Humanist education utilized the Greek ideal of balance between physical and mental development, Quintilian's ideal of the well-informed orator able and ready to devote himself to public service, and Christian faith. Unfortunately, in practice, slavish devotion to exercises in grammar and rhetoric was often substituted for the classical spirit, memorization for appreciation, and whipping for the desire to emulate the ancient heroes.

The continued growth and development of the emerging nation-states called for a type of training which, while clearly within the Humanist tradition, tended to emphasize those parts of Humanism particularly suited to success at court and in government service. The difficulty lay not so much with the theory of Humanistic education as with the practice. For the politician, the courtier, the man of affairs, the bookish learning of grammar school and university was insufficient and much of it unnecessary. Whereas the Middle Ages had separated the education of clerk and knight, it was necessary for the modern man of affairs to combine them. There was, as Ascham put it in *The Scholemaster,* a new inclination "to join learning with comely exercises." Most important, perhaps, was a powerful utilitarian urge. New subjects were becoming not only desirable but essential to the man of action. For those who stood behind the soldiers and made war and peace, for diplomats, politicians, and statesmen, the vernacular, history, and geography were becoming of increasing importance.

The scholar-gentlemen

The ideal of the scholar-gentleman was best set out in *Il Cortegiano* (The Courtier) by the Italian Count Baldassare Castiglione. The book, first appearing in print in 1532, represented the observations of a lifetime spent in the service of Italian princes. It presented in detail the character and qualities of the ideal courtier—the man of action engaged in the service of a prince, on the field of battle as well as in the council chambers, the man completely at home in the society of both gentlemen and ladies. He must be trained in the use of arms and in horsemanship, courageous, but not a bully or braggart. He must know Latin and Greek in addition to his native tongue. Sports, games, and recreation must be cultivated and some proficiency at such things as swimming, hunting, tennis, music, drawing, painting, and chess. In all these pursuits he must seek to excel, for the Renaissance exalted individual accomplishments, but the pursuit of excellence must be carried on with propriety and decorum, although, to paraphrase Alfred N. Whitehead's observation, it was often a pursuit by bandits. Castiglione's book represented the Renaissance in its most human, vibrant form, and it became a classic statement of the alternative that might be offered to both medieval Scholasticism and the narrow linguistic education that Humanism offered in practice.

While catching the spirit of Castiglione's courtier, the northern Renaissance never was quite so carried away with aesthetic interests or attention to fair ladies as were the Italians. In *The Boke named the Governour,* Sir Thomas Elyot wrote an educational treatise prescribing the training needed by the English nobility. It was basically a Humanistic education in the classics, with ample play for the interests of the student if he sought recreation in music, painting, or sculpture. In addition, there was to be a variety of exercises for the health and perfection of the body. Elyot enumerated at length the "vertue in manners"— affability, placability, mercy, benevolence, and so forth—that must accompany the perfection of language and bodily development in the true gentleman. A thoroughgoing aristocrat, Elyot had no doubt that the nobility's natural superiority and ability to rule demanded a special educational program. While utilitarian considerations motivated the development of the total scheme, classical precedents were sought as confirmation for the thesis that particular character traits or physical and artistic pastimes were truly suitable for one of gentle birth. Indeed, Elyot's treatise bears a striking resemblance to the Greek essay *On the Training of Children* attributed to Plutarch.

While writing on the proper education of the courtier was a favorite pastime of many scholar-statesmen during the sixteenth century, some of them had little experience in applying their theories in the actual instruction of prospective governors. One who did, however, was Roger Ascham (1515–1568), a tutor to the future Elizabeth I and other children of nobility, a classical scholar at Cambridge, and, as Latin secretary both to Queen Mary and to Queen Elizabeth, a practicing courtier. While his major work, *The Scholemaster,* does not spell out the ideal of the courtier as completely as the writings of Castiglione or Elyot, it is more instructive as to the teaching procedures that were used in training young aristocrats.

Ascham's method

The teaching situation experienced by Ascham and other tutors to the children of the nobility was quite different from that of the grammar school master dealing with a roomful of students. Tutorial instruction—one teacher working with one student—was the rule. Ascham employed the method of double-translation to instruct students in the study of language, the most fundamental part of the education of a courtier. While it was not unique at the time, his application of the theory of imitation was crucial in determining his methodology. He desired to train his students to write like Cicero, but he believed that this could not be done by directly copying Cicero or by studying those who had been his most able imitators. Rather, the student should study how Cicero had imitated Plato, Isocrates, Demosthenes, and other Greeks. One could become another Cicero by following the same models according to the same principles as Cicero himself had done. In order to understand how to follow or to imitate Cicero, one must first observe how Cicero imitated the Greeks.

The method to be used in comparing two authors was as follows:

> But if a man would take this pain also when he hath laid two places of Homer and Virgil, or of Demosthenes and Tully together, to teach plainly withal after this sort.
> 1. Tully retaineth thus much of the matter, these sentences, these words.
> 2. This and that he leaveth out, which he doth wittily to this end and purpose.
> 3. This he addeth here.
> 4. This he diminisheth there.
> 5. This he ordereth thus, with placing that here, not there.
> 6. This he altereth and changeth, either in property of words, in form of sentence, in substance of the matter, or in one or other convenient circumstance of the author's present purpose. In these few rude English words are wrapt up all the necessary tools and instruments wherewith true imitation is rightly wrought withal in any tongue (Ascham, 1900, pp. 137–138).

Ascham acknowledged that his method was "not of mine own forging, but partly left unto me by the cunningest master and one of the worthiest gentlemen that ever England bred, Sir John Cheke, partly borrowed by me out of the shop of the dearest friend I have out of England, Io. St. [Johann Sturm]" (Ascham, 1900, p. 138). Cheke, a noted Cambridge scholar, had been Ascham's master at St. John's College, while Ascham and Sturm corresponded for many years concerning Sturm's famous Latin gymnasium at Strasbourg. The method which all three men advocated and Ascham chose to call double-translation was very similar to that proposed for studying Greek by Cicero himself in *De Oratore*.

Ascham began the study of language by having the very young pupil memorize the first part of the grammar in the manner typical of the period. "After the child hath learned perfectly the eight parts of speech, let him then learn the right joining together of substantives with adjectives, the noun with the verb, the relative with the antecedent" (Ascham, 1900, p. 11). But the student should avoid actually speaking Latin and writing Latin prose until a good deal of the language had been learned. This was contrary to the procedure then used in the grammar schools.

> And in learning farther his syntax by mine advice, he shall not use the common order in common schools for making of Latins, whereby the child commonly learneth: first, an evil choice of words (and right choice of words, saith Caesar, is the foundation of eloquence) than a wrong placing of words; and lastly, an ill framing of the sentence, with a perverse judgment both of words and sentences. These faults, taking once root in youth, be never or hardly plucked away in age. Moreover, there is no one thing that hath more either dulled the wits or taken away the will of children from learning than the care they have to satisfy their masters in making of Latins (Ascham, 1900, p. 11).

By using his method of double-translation, Ascham believed he could teach the pupil grammar and perfect style without introducing the bad habits encouraged by the popular system. He seemed not to be disturbed by the possibility that all inclination toward originality might also be stifled.

> The way is this. After the three Concordances learned, as I touched before, let the master read unto him the Epistles of Cicero, gathered together and chosen out by Sturmius, for the capacity of children.
>
> First, let him teach the child cheerfully and plainly the cause and matter of the letter, then let him construe it into English, so oft as the child may easily carry away the understanding of it; lastly, parse it over perfectly. This done thus, let the child by-and-by both construe and parse it over again, so that it may appear that the child doubteth in nothing that his master taught him before. After this the child must take a paper book, and sitting in some place, where no man shall prompt him, by himself, let him translate into English his former lesson. Then showing it to his master, let the master take from him his Latin book, and pausing an hour at the least, then

let the child translate his own English into Latin again in another paper book. When the child bringeth it turned into Latin, the master must compare it with Tully's book, and lay them both together, and where the child doth well, either in choosing or true placing of Tully's words, let the master praise him and say here ye do well. For I assure you there is no such whetstone to sharpen a good wit and encourage a will to learning as his praise.

But if the child miss either in forgetting a word or in changing a good with a worse, or misordering the sentence, I would not have the master either frown or chide with him, if the child have done his diligence, and used no truantship therein. For I know by good experience that a child shall take more profit of two faults, gently warned of, than of four things rightly hit. For then the master shall have good occasion to say unto him, Tully would have used such a word, not this; Tully would have placed this word here, not there; would have used this case, this number, this person, this degree, this gender; he would have used this mood, this tense, this simple rather than this compound; this adverb here, not there; he would have ended the sentence with this verb, not with that noun or participle, etc. (Ascham, 1900, pp. 12–14).

The method was quite simple. The tutor construed and parsed the passage, and the student immediately repeated it to make certain that he knew the lesson. When this had been verified, the student then wrote out the English translation which, after an interval, he attempted to translate back into the original Latin. Each student was checked individually, and the sole emphasis was upon a precise reproduction of the model. If this procedure were followed, the student would learn his *Syntax* through the usage of the best writers, using grammar only to deal with difficult points as they arose in study. No attempt was made to construct original Latin prose by using the rules of grammar as a guide in fitting words together. Instead, speaking and writing were learned by employing the phraseology of the finest exemplars. The cultivation of errors was thought to be impossible because none were permitted to enter. At some point the pupil was given a book of godly morality written in excellent Latin. By this means the student improved his Latin and his character simultaneously.

After double-translation, Ascham insisted that the student note six points.

> But to go forward as you perceive your scholar to go better and better on away, first with understanding his lesson more quickly, with parsing more readily, with translating more speedily and perfectly than he was wont, after give him longer lessons to translate, and withal begin to teach him both in nouns and verbs what is *Proprium,* and what is *Translatum,* what *Synonymum,* what *Diversum,* which be *Contraria,* and which be most notable phrases in all his lecture. . . .
> Your scholar then must have the third paper book: In the which, after he hath done his double translation, let him write after this sort four of these forenamed six, diligently marked out of every lesson:—

Quatuor.
{
Propria.
Translata.
Synonyma.
Diversa.
Contraria.
Phrases.
}

＊   ＊   ＊

> This diligent translating, joined with this heedful marking, in the aforesaid epistles, and afterward in some plain oration of Tully, as *pro lege Manilia, pro Archia Poeta,* or in those three *ad C. Caes.,* shall work such a right choice of words, so straight a framing of sentences, such a true judgment, both to write skilfully and speak wittily, as wise men shall both praise and marvel at (Ascham, 1900, pp. 17–19).

When the student has mastered translating and marking the six points,

> . . . I would have him read now a good deal at every lecture; for he shall not now use daily translation, but only construe again, and pass, where ye suspect is any need. Yet let him not omit in these books his former exercise, in marking diligently and writing orderly out his six points. And for translating, use you yourself every second or third day to choose out some Epistle *ad Atticum,* some notable commonplace out of his Orations, or some other part of Tully, by your discretion, which your

scholar may not know where to find; and translate it you yourself into plain natural English, and then give it him to translate into Latin again; allowing him good space and time to do it both with diligent heed and good advisement. . . . When he bringeth it translated unto you, bring you forth the place of Tully; lay them together; compare the one with the other: commend his good choice and right placing of words; show his faults gently, but blame them not over-sharply . . . (Ascham, 1900, p. 94).

In this more advanced stage the student was not required to double-translate all the authors because some of the writing was not truly classic, but the matter of style still had to be based on Tully. The student, working from a translation "into plain natural English" of an unfamiliar passage from Tully, had to select from memory the words of Tully that corresponded to the English translation.

If a student had successfully completed these two stages in which perfect imitation was demanded, a final phase involving some degree of original composition was permitted.

When by this diligent and speedy reading over those fore-named good books of Tully, Terence, Caesar, and Livy, and by this second kind of translating out of your English, time shall breed skill, and use shall bring perfection, then ye may try, if you will, your scholar with the third kind of translation, although the two first ways by mine opinion be not only sufficient of themselves, but also surer, both for the master's teaching and scholar's learning, than this third way is, which is thus: Write you in English some letter, as it were from him to his father, or to some other friend, naturally, according to the disposition of the child, or some tale, or fable, or plain narration, according as Aphthonius beginneth his exercises of learning, and let him translate it into Latin again, abiding in such place where no other scholar may prompt him. But yet use yourself such discretion for choice therein as the matter may be within the compass, both for words and sentences, of his former learning and reading. And now take heed lest your scholar do not better in some point than you yourself, except ye have been diligently exercised in these kinds of translating before (Ascham, 1900, pp. 96–97).

In the second stage, then, the student was given an English translation of a Latin passage he had not seen. By analogy with what he had already learned, he had to reproduce the Latin exactly. But he was not to bother with the parsing and construction of the Latin unless difficulties arose. In this way the analytical was eliminated as much as possible in favor of the imitative. Ascham seemed to admit the third stage, where some originality was feasible, only very reluctantly. A stylist through and through, Ascham was interested in imitative purity of form almost to the point of completely ignoring content. His caution to the teacher to beware of the student being more able than the master is a revealing commentary on the competence of teachers at the time.

Discipline and individual differences

Ascham had a good deal to say about disciplining students, for he felt that it had a considerable bearing on interest and motivation. He repeatedly urged the tutor to be cheerful and not to "frown or chide . . . if the child have done his diligence, and used no truantship therein" (Ascham, 1900, p. 13). This emphasis on effort rather than immediate achievement was consistent with his championing of the "hard wit" as contrasted with the "quick wit."

Without the benefit of modern experiments in reinforcement of learning, Ascham was convinced that praise was a more powerful teacher than punishment. ". . . where the child doth well . . . let the master praise him and say here ye do well. For I assure you there is no such whetstone to sharpen a good wit and encourage a will to learning as his praise" (Ascham, 1900, p. 13). And gentleness should be exercised when correction did seem necessary: "If your scholar do miss sometimes . . . chide not hastily, for that shall both dull his wit and discourage his diligence, but monish him gently, which shall make him both willing to amend, and glad to go forward in love and hope of learning" (Ascham, 1900, p. 19).

In one brief passage, Ascham contrasted his theory of discipline with that which was widely accepted in the contemporary schools. "In mine opinion," he wrote, "love is fitter than fear, gentleness better than beating, to bring up a child rightly in learning" (Ascham, 1900, p. 19). At a time when the effectiveness of a master was often measured by the frequency and severity of the whippings he administered, Ascham contended that

> . . . even the wisest of your great beaters do as oft punish nature as they do correct faults. Yea, many times the better nature is sorely punished; for, if one, by quickness of wit, take his lesson readily, another, by hardness of wit, taketh it not so speedily, the first is always commended, the other is commonly punished; when a wise schoolmaster should rather discretely consider the right disposition of both their natures, and not so much way [weigh] what either of them is able to do now, as what either of them is likely to do hereafter (Ascham, 1900, p. 20).

If the governing families would only follow Socrates' advice and teach their children "by playing and pleasure" rather than "by compulsion and fear," they would find young gentlemen running as willingly to school as they do to the stable. "They find fear and bondage in schools, they feel liberty and freedom in stables; which causeth them utterly to abhor the one and most gladly to haunt the other" (Ascham, 1900, p. 36).

Although Ascham never had to deal with the problem which confronts teachers in a mass democracy of instructing a random sample of "all the children of all the people" in one classroom (indeed, the very thought might have repelled him), he developed a theory of individual differences while tutoring the children of nobility. He complained that neither tutors nor parents knew how to recognize true "wit," that is, real intelligence and aptness for learning. Too many masters favored the quick-witted prodigy and chastised as indolent the child who learned slowly. Yet "hard wits," those who are less pliable and less ready to jump at new suggestions but are not "over dull" or "lumpish," often prove the best scholars in the long run. In comparing these two kinds of intellectual capacity in children, the master should be discreet enough to "not so much way [weigh] what either of them is able to do now, as what either of them is likely to do hereafter." Recent research indicates that teachers continue to be unduly impressed by the student who responds quickly. Much of our teaching procedure, particularly the testing process, rewards speed rather than thorough understanding. This tendency is apparently particularly harmful in the teaching of the culturally disadvantaged child.

The chief fault of "quick wits" is flightiness; they are "soon hot, and desirous of this and that; as cold and soon weary of the same again." They are also "very ready of disposition to be carried over quickly, by any light company, to any riot and unthriftiness when they be young." In contrast, "hard wits" usually prove the best in the long run, just as with "wood and stone, not the softest, but hardest, be always aptest for portraiture, both fairest for pleasure, and most durable for profit" (Ascham, 1900, pp. 20–24). Obviously, young men possessing the stable and morally sound qualities of the "hard wit" could be trusted in the capacity of governors while the "quick wits" would be dangerous. While Ascham was undoubtedly sincere in his admonition to parents and tutors, the practices of courtiers often were more in keeping with his characterization of the "quick" than the "hard wit." The records leave little doubt that many were corrupt, immoral, and opportunistic. Even Ascham, in his middle years, after spending some time at court, found it difficult to choose between the frugal, quiet life of the scholar and the noisy, colorful, but often decadent life at court.

Ironically, Ascham apparently turned out to be one of those quick wits "that show forth fair blossoms and broad leaves in spring time, but bring out small and not long lasting fruit in harvest time; and that only such as fall and rot before they be ripe, and so never, or seldom, come to any good at all" (Ascham, 1900, p. 22). He showed great promise in his early years at Cambridge and was justified in his expectations of receiving a choice appointment at that institution. But, although he counted as friends monarchs, cardinals, scholars, and other persons of fame or fortune and did teach at Cambridge for many years, he never received the appointment he sought so diligently. Instead, he was tormented by missed opportunities and meager financial means during much of his life. He was forever seeking patronage and flattering those who might do him favors. He attempted to combine the careers of academician, courtier, and author and missed greatness in each field. There is a striking similarity between Ascham's career and that of the professor who in our time tries to combine the functions of teacher, government servant, and author of popular books on scholarly subjects.

While *The Scholemaster* was immediately popular and had considerable influence on English education for at least a century after its appearance in 1570, Ascham's other noted work, *Toxophilus, the schoole of shootinge conteyned in two bookes*, remains one of the classic statements of the sport of archery. It represented the concern of the courtier for physical fitness and care of the body, and demonstrated that it was seemly for someone who saw himself as a scholar of Latin and Greek to devote his energies to a treatise on such a subject.

The great importance of participation in the social life at court made it necessary that "young gentlemen should use and delight in all courtly exercises and gentlemanlike exercises."

> Therefore, to ride comely; to run fair at the tilt or ring; to play at all weapons; to shoot fair in bow or surely in gun; to vault lustily; to run, to leap, to wrestle, to swim; to dance comely; to sing, and play of instruments cunningly; to hawk, to hunt, to play at tennis, and all pastimes generally, which be joined with labour, used in open place, and on the daylight containing either some fit exercise for war, or some pleasant pastime for peace, be not only comely and decent, but also very necessary, for a courtly gentlemen to use (Ascham, 1900, p. 63).

While it was held that all these pastimes were necessary for character development, bodily exercise, or defense of the realm, it appears that some were also useful for achieving excellence in the more sensuous pursuits of court life.

Ascham, in keeping with Humanist doctrine and the notion of the true gentleman, devoted a major part of *The Scholemaster* to urging tutors and parents to instill virtue and manners in the young. It was important that they be kept "in God's fear" so that they might serve God and the commonwealth well. In the Humanist view of education, moral excellence outranked intellectual achievement. Even the tutor was to be chosen principally for his goodness of character and "if he be also learned, he is the more commendable" (Elyot, 1883, I, 36). The student was to acquire the proper sense of morality and conduct through three means: the imitation and observation of the tutor, exposure to the advice and examples contained in ancient literature, and Biblical study. While Elyot was concerned that a proper nurse be found for the newborn infant so that his morality would be protected, Ascham felt that the most dangerous period was from seventeen to twenty-seven when "they have commonly the rein of all license in their own hand, and specially such as do live in the court" (Ascham, 1900, p. 45).

Ascham was very firm in his conviction that experience was not the best teacher. "An unhappy master he is that is made cunning by many shipwrecks; a miserable merchant, that is neither rich nor wise but after some bankruptcies. It is costly wisdom that is bought by experience" (Ascham, 1900, pp. 58–59). Experience was profitable only after proper preparation in learning. Formal education, when joined with honest exercise and pastimes, gave a complete preparation for dealing with whatever might be encountered in life. Once the student had attained some linguistic proficiency through much *translatio linguarum*, imitation was to "bring forth more learning and breed up truer judgment, than any other exercise that can be used." In every action, whether it be using a bow, addressing a lady, or composing a Latin verse, the courtier was trained for strict conformity to a prescribed model.

While Ascham and his fellow scholar-courtiers did much to relieve the hard lot of Shakespeare's

> Whining schoolboy, with his satchel
> And Shining morning face, creeping like snail
> Unwillingly to school

the response, particularly among schoolmasters, was not always favorable. Richard Mulcaster, a noted headmaster and contemporary of Ascham, derided the notions of abandoning whippings. and motivating students by making the study of language enjoyable. While he conceded that this might be possible in tutoring the children of the aristocracy, Mulcaster was convinced that gentleness was inappropriate in a "public" grammar school.

The education of the courtier was, of course, class education intended for the very few, and it was dependent on the existence of a particular social-political situation. It suffered from a slowly encroaching rigidity that created a widening gulf between theory and practice. Within a half-century after the publication of *The Scholemaster*, Francis Bacon pointed out the two "distempers of learning" that had developed in the system: the emptiness of mere words and style, and the folly of theory unrelated to material reality. He noted that

> . . . these four causes concurring, viz., 1. admiration of the ancients; 2. enmity to the schoolmen; 3. an exact study of language; and, 4. a desire of powerful preaching—introduced an affected study of eloquence and copiousness of speech, which then began to flourish. This soon grew to excess, insomuch that men studied more after words than matter, more after the choiceness of phrase, and the round and neat composition . . . than after the weight of matter, dignity of subject, soundness of argument, life of invention, or depth of judgment. . . . then did Car and Ascham, in their lectures and writings, almost deify Cicero and Demosthenes. . . .
>
> The second disease is worse in its nature than the former. . . . For the human mind, if it acts upon matter, and contemplates the nature of things, and the works of God, operates according to the stuff, and is limited thereby; but if it works upon itself, as the spider does, then it has no end; but produces cobwebs of learning, admirable indeed for the fineness of the thread, but of no substance or profit (Bacon, 1900, pp. 15–17).

Ascham had written *The Scholemaster* out of a concern for the deplorable conditions he found in the schools of his day. They were not providing the governing class with prerequisites essential for the performance of their duties. Now Bacon was leveling a similar charge at Ascham and his contemporaries. Their curriculum and methods failed to meet the demands of a new time.

The Jesuits, Masters of Method

The Church was challenged by the charm of pagan learning, on the one hand, and by the shock of the Reformation, on the other. One of its responses to these challenges was a system of schools which moved Francis Bacon to make the oft-quoted remark: "For the doctrine of school-learning, it were the shortest way to refer it to the Jesuits, who, in point of usefulness, have herein excelled" (*Advancement of Learning*, 1900, p. 207).

The Jesuit schools are selected for discussion not because of their originality in content, form, or even spirit, but because they illustrate how schooling can be organized and systematized to make materials, methods of instruction, and teachers uniformly effective over broad regions of space and time.

The Jesuits systematized every phase of schoolkeeping. Motivation, presentation, practice, and testing were reduced to rules and precepts. These were brought together in the *Ratio Studiorum*, issued first in 1586 and then in revised form in 1599. An example of the thoroughness and definiteness of the directions is afforded by the following quotation:

> If an oration or poem is being explained, first its meaning must be explained, if it is obscure, and the various interpretations considered. Second, the whole method of the workmanship, whether invention, disposition, or delivery is to be considered, also how aptly the author ingratiates himself, how appropriately he speaks, or from what topics he takes his material for persuading, for ornament, or for moving his audience; how many precepts he unites in one and the same place, by what method he includes with the figures of thought the means of instilling belief, and again the figures of thought which he weaves into the figures of words. Third, some passages similar in subject-matter and expression to be adduced and other orators or poets who have used the same precept for the sake of proving or narrating something similar are to be cited. Fourth, let the facts be confirmed by statements of authorities, if opportunity offers. Fifth, let statements from history, from mythology, and from all erudition be sought which illustrate the passage. At last, let the words be considered carefully, and their fitness, their elegance, their number, and their rhythm noted. However, let these things be considered, not that the master may always dis-

cuss everything, but that from them he may select those which are most fitting.[1]

Jesuit activity in education also illustrates how a movement not originally established for instruction used it to achieve its goals. To be a militant force for the Church, the movement needed leaders who could counter the Reformation on intellectual as well as religious grounds. Such leaders had to be trained, and to secure a considerable number of them, a method of teacher training was indispensable. Under these circumstances, it was natural for the problem of method to become an object of deliberate study. It marked another step in the emergence of teaching as a rationally based art.

Rivalry as motivation

The faith in classical Humanistic schooling is puzzling to our times. How could young people become enthusiastic enough about ancient Greek heroes to study Greek language and literature? We can account for this enthusiasm only by the fact that the revival of learning was not merely an intellectual phenomenon, but also marked the captivation of an era by a style of life that has managed to fascinate Western man in every era, namely, the Greek ideal of man. When people are thus fascinated, they desire to emulate the model, and when the model places high value on individual self-cultivation, on individual excellence, rivalry becomes the mode of school motivation *par excellence*. In such circumstances schoolboys will compete for whatever the cultural milieu designates as the marks of excellence, provided the school can translate these marks into school behavior.

Rivalry was instituted by the Jesuit schoolmasters between members of a class, between groups within a class, and between classes. Classes were divided into armies, e.g., of Romans and Carthaginians, and pupils were given military ranks. With somewhat incomplete fidelity to the military model, a private who bested an officer in a scholastic exercise assumed the rank of the vanquished.

---

[1] From *St. Ignatius and the Ratio Studiorum,* by E. A. Fitzpatrick, pp. 212–213. Copyright 1933, McGraw-Hill Book Company. Used by permission.

Even more important methodologically was the use of rivalry as a teaching device. Each pupil had a rival charged with catching every mistake he made and correcting it. Not only did the individual's rank depend on alertness and adequate preparation of every lesson, but his team's fortunes also depended on it (Fitzpatrick, 1933, p. 203).

Once a year, two or three of the best scholars in a class were matched against a team from the class above it on subject matter common to both. It would be interesting to know whether the results of such interclass competition revealed facts about class placement as embarrassing as those disclosed by our achievement tests.

Public exhibitions of scholastic skill at declamation and debate were encouraged, but only for those who were trained for it. The master was to polish essays to be given in public, although he was not to write the essay or compose the speech himself.

Most important. of all was the praise of the teacher consistently reinforcing every desirable response and his disapproval no less consistently discouraging undesirable deviation.

When these methods failed, as with all but angels they occasionally must, there was admonition and punishment. One rule of the *Ratio* points out that it is better for the teacher to pretend not to have seen certain class misdeeds, if they can be overlooked without disadvantage (Fitzpatrick, 1933, p. 206). It takes a long time for the new teacher to realize that not all misdeeds are directed to flouting his authority; that while some are designed to test it, many others merely fill the mysterious need of children to erupt when congregated in classrooms.

Another example of psychological wisdom is the provision that a teacher never strike a pupil, but leave such punishment to an official Corrector, "who is not of the Society." In other words, dissociate the punishing act from the teaching act. No less insightful are the injunctions not to make sarcastic remarks or speak discourteously to pupils; not to call pupils by anything but their right names; not to excuse pupils from class for public exhibitions and plays; not to play favorites; not to speak to pupils outside of class except briefly and then only on serious matters, such conversations to be held in an open place and not in the classroom; not to use pupils as copyists; and not to permit pupils to spend their own money for the school.

Methods of presentation and exercise

The prelection was the chief method of presentation. The teacher in effect studied the assignment aloud in front of the class, and the class was expected to repeat his performance as faithfully as possible. The prelection was adapted to the various tasks to be performed: translating Greek materials to Latin or translating either of them to the vernacular; criticizing or appreciating a selection from a Latin or Greek author; or giving the directions for writing a composition or expounding a theological question.

Perhaps more significant for method was the way the teacher secured overlapping review. Every segment of instruction was reviewed almost immediately after its completion. The master's prelection, the week's work, the term's work, the year's work were all reviewed. Each Saturday there was a review of the week's work, and for general promotion, students were given a thorough repetition of all the main points of the year's work. It was a methodical attempt to secure learning and overlearning by taking advantage of the curve of forgetting (Fitzpatrick, 1933, pp. 200–201).

Assignments were regular. Written work was to be handed in by all grammar scholars every day but Saturday. In some classes verse exercises in Latin were handed in twice a week and a Greek theme once a week. These exercises were corrected by the master, or by pupils exchanging papers, or by the pupil himself from a model furnished by the master. Student helpers were appointed to watch over the pupils and to report faults or defaults in the preparation of lessons.

The disputation was retained in some subjects. Students were encouraged to make objections to points in the prelection and to raise them with the master or to reserve them for a disputation. With respect to presiding over a disputation the *Ratio* advised that the master

> . . . preside in such a way that he may himself seem to take part on both sides . . . he shall not keep silent too long, nor yet speak all the time, but let the pupils set forth what they know; he shall . . . not permit an objec-

tion which is practically answered to be pressed too far, nor an answer which is unsound to stand too long; after a discussion, he shall briefly define and explain the entire matter (Fitzpatrick, 1933, p. 144).

The Jesuits left little undone in their efforts to make learning unavoidable, and to frustrate this attempt the pupil would have had to be very stupid or unusually intelligent.

How are the methods of the Jesuits—or more generally, the methods in vogue at the best of the classical Humanistic schools and colleges—to be evaluated? If well-developed habits of speaking, writing, thinking, and judging are valid objectives, these schools achieved them brilliantly by means of a compact curriculum made up of ". . . the human letters of the different tongues, and logic, natural and moral philosophy, metaphysics, theology, both scholastic and positive, and Sacred Scriptures" (Fitzpatrick, 1933, p. 21).

It was a course of study made up largely of linguistic materials taught for overlearning in a highly prestructured form, but that it resulted in rote learning only, as has so often been charged, is doubtful. The more just observation is that the materials of the curriculum had a built-in logic and a built-in set of values. Pupils learned words, to be sure, but these words structured their selective process so that they became *forms* of experience rather than specific responses reinstated on cue. Nor were the words merely logical pigeonholes. The classical literatures clothed the words with imagery and peopled the boy's experience with a cast of characters who acted out the human drama with impressive directness and vividness.

So long as Western culture conceived excellence in literary terms and religious categories, the methods of the Jesuits were successful. When success came to be expressed in terms of technology and industrial power, literary accomplishments, rhetorical skill, and self-cultivation on the Greek model became anachronistic and with them the school designed to accomplish these results.

Chapter VII

TEACHING ACCORDING TO NATURE: COMENIUS

While the classical Humanistic schools were flourishing, the learning materials relevant to the new science, the new modes of production, new geographical discoveries, and new political forces were being born and nurtured in the minds of scholars. These materials, however, did not immediately find a place in the curriculum of the schools, for it is a long road between the research frontier of scholarship and the classroom. At their best educationists travel back and forth along this road, but the run-of-the-mill school changes its ways and lessons slowly. For one thing, the relevance of new knowledge is not always apparent to the textbook maker. For another, the teacher is not in a position to assimilate this knowledge readily. Finally, new materials tend to be fitted into old objectives, and when they resist this amalgamation, their ingression into the curriculum is delayed.

Of all these factors, the last was perhaps the most important. The empirical knowledge derived from systematic observation and the theoretical knowledge developed in mathematics and the physical sciences differ radically from the literary materials of the Humanistic schools. After the Renaissance, the new outlooks and the new contents did knock, albeit hesitantly, on the doors of the school. The emphasis on observation of real objects, usefulness of knowledge in daily life, and personal religious freedom eventually made itself felt in the school, but for a long time it manifested itself under the old objectives, namely, to teach Latin and Greek more easily and more effectively. The work of Johann Amos Comenius (Komensky) (1592–1670) is an interesting example of how new wines were put into old bottles, i.e., into Latin school books, a task "from which he had so often turned in disgust" (Keatinge, 1896, p. 91).

The life of the man was a mixture of idealism, vision, mysticism, calamity, courage, and tragedy. Born in Nivnitz, Moravia, he was the third child and only son of a miller who was a member of the Moravian Brethren, a Hussite sect. At the age of 12 he was orphaned and shortly thereafter because his guardians misappropriated his inheritance he was penniless. He had the usual elementary and Latin school training. At the Latin school he is said to have applied himself diligently enough to earn the middle name of Amos (Spinka, 1943, p. 27), but he apparently noted shortcomings in the methods of instruction to which he was subjected.

His higher education, in preparation for the ministry, was received at the University of Herborn in Nassau. In 1613 he matriculated at the University of Heidelberg, where he studied astronomy and read some of the work of Copernicus. He was ordained in 1616. At Herborn Comenius met John Henry Alsted, a Calvinistic theologian who was interested in educational reform and apparently influenced Comenius considerably. After his training was over, Comenius returned to Moravia where he served as the chief Bishop of the Moravian Brethren, but also taught school and wrote a number of books. As a result of the Thirty Years' War, he suffered exile, loss of his family, and persecution, but his work as a schoolmaster continued in Poland, Prussia, Hungary, and Sweden. At one time, there was talk of establishing a college based on his principles in England (1641–1642), and he was supposed to have been called to the presidency of Harvard University (Spinka, 1943, p. 86). He died in 1670 in Amsterdam having impaired his reputation by involvement with a number of religious visionaries who regarded themselves as prophets.

Today Comenius is read and studied as an educational statesman whose theories reflected a vision of human unity and dignity more appropriate to our day than to his. Yet it was as a writer of textbooks and an organizer of schools that he was known and respected in his own day.

In 1658 at Nuremburg appeared *Orbis Sensualium Pictus*

with the subtitle: *A World of Things Obvious to the Senses Drawn in Pictures.* It was the first school picture book ever printed, the historians tell us, and hugely successful, running through many editions, one coming out in New York as late as 1810. Other texts written or projected by John Amos Comenius included:

The *Janua Linguarum Reserata* or *The Gate of Languages Unlocked,* the first of the series to be published (1631). The *Orbis* was a simplified version of this book, and the *Vestibulum* was supposed to be an introduction to it. The *Janua* was made up of 8,000 or so Latin words arranged in 1,000 simple sentences with matching vernacular translations in parallel columns. It included information on a wide variety of subjects.

The *Vestibulum,* an introductory first reader, was made up of several hundred sentences utilizing the most commonly used Latin words, each with its translation in an opposite column.

The *Atrium,* an elaboration of the *Janua,* featured Latin-Latin vocabulary rather than Latin-vernacular.

The *Thesaurus* graded extracts from easy Latin authors to furnish reading material for the upper three years of the school (Cubberley, 1920a, pp. 412–413).

"The Great Didactic"

In 1627 Comenius began his work on *The Great Didactic.* Although it was probably completed in 1632, it was not printed in its original Czech until 1849. A Latin translation with several additional chapters was brought out in Amsterdam in 1657 as the first part of his *Opera Didactica Omnia.* It is in this work that the theoretical foundation of his educational schemes was developed.

In a way, the theory followed simply and directly from his religious belief in the unity of all men in God and the unity of all things as the creation of God. *Ergo,* all knowledge was of a piece and to know less than all was to have an incomplete awareness of God. Hence the notion of pansophism in which all men were to learn all things in ever-widening spirals of complexity and generality as they grew from infancy to adulthood.

In *The Great Didactic* Comenius expounded a system of universal education based on certain principles of learning reared in turn on what he regarded as principles of natural development. Comenius has been praised for being a forerunner of those espousing a truly democratic vision of the common school and for providing an insight into the educational process that was not to be appreciated for generations. But Comenius' influence and fame were measured in his day, at least, by a set of textbooks to be used in teaching Latin.

Language and Knowledge

The texts incorporated some of the new sciences and reflected an interest in the common objects of ordinary experience as against the experience of ancient Greek and Roman figures of exalted station. They also reflected the stress on observation in the new science, which pointed to sense perception as the fountain of all genuine, as distinguished from merely verbal, knowledge. *Orbis Pictus*, for example, refers to the world, the heavens, fire, birds, cattle, flesh and bowels, cookery, butchery, eclipses, geometry, printing, and a score of other categories. In the process of learning Latin, the pupil, if Comenius had his way, would also learn *about* his natural environment and the activities of common life. The pictures, of course, were to serve as surrogates for direct perception of the things themselves.

The idea of incorporating content in language study was not new. Even the notion that content might be used to engage the interest of the reluctant scholar was tried by Egbert (*c.* 1022–1024), who composed 2,473 lines of verse in his *Fecundia Ratis* to interest boys. The lines, which grew progressively more difficult, touched on material from the Bible, Latin prose, and Latin poetry. In the eleventh century, Latin readers relied heavily on fables full of allusions to incidents in the life and manners of the time, e.g., *Fabulae et Parabaloe* of Odo of Cerrington (*c.* 1200), a collection of fables edited by Ernest Voigt (Abelson, 1906, p. 19). It was in the kind of information and its extent that Comenius' texts represented an important advance.

Comenius' texts were not merely collections of informational items. For example, in *Orbis Pictus* one section is called "The Barber's Shop." There is a picture of such a shop in which a dozen objects and operations are depicted and numbered. The phrases in Latin and the vernacular paired in parallel columns refer to these objects. Each section had its "core" theme, so to speak.

The Order of Nature

The book was part of a series. The series as a whole and each book in the series embodied certain pedagogical principles fully described in *The Great Didactic*. One such principle was that Nature in its formative processes begins with the universal and ends with the particular. Pedagogically, this was interpreted by Comenius to mean that instruction ought to begin with such first principles as one can find in a subject, and that these should be exemplified in ever-increasing detail. Each topic, accordingly, would be studied at every stage of development but in ever greater detail. In this way all men could come to know all things (Comenius, 1657, XVI, sec. 45; Keatinge, 1896, p. 274).

Comenius' method leans heavily on the order of Nature. Nature has its own reasons, its own timetable, and its own means for bringing seed to fruition, as anyone familiar with biological change can hardly fail to note. Indeed, the way in which plants and animals follow timetables of development that are impressively uniform for members of the species, and for each species over enormous spans of time, is one of the most formidable obstacles to a mechanical interpretation of Nature, because it points to a genic code that limits tolerable variations both in number and in degree. Paradoxically perhaps, the more evidence one finds for such a code—and biology is finding such evidence—the more sense it makes to speak of living things developing according to a plan or purpose, but a purpose that is encoded "mechanically" by each organism in the genes.

Because the order of development is "natural," that is, not contrived by any human being, it has the connotation of rightness, as the edict of a power greater than and certainly independent of any human being. In other words, the natural order is not only descriptive of what does happen but is also prescriptive of what should happen. Plato and Aristotle incorporated this type of thinking into a theory about the psychic and moral life of the individual and of the good society. With respect to the social order, this prescriptive aspect of nature is conceived as "natural law"; with respect to the individual, as a fixed human nature.

The theoretical difficulties with this notion are notorious, chiefly because the prescriptions of Nature are so diversely construed by men in different cultures. This has seriously undermined belief in the concept of natural law. But whether there can be a science of human behavior if there are no uniformities and invariant relationships in such behavior is a question no less formidable. Even if the statements of science about human behavior are only probable, what makes one statement more probable than another? Surely, it is because it predicts what will happen more reliably than its rivals.

Comenius was arguing from the analogy between plant life and human life, and insofar as human life is like that of plants, one can expect illuminating suggestions for understanding the growth of children. Unfortunately, the differences between human life and plant life are far more important for the study of mankind than are the resemblances, and this wreaks havoc with the analogy. A few examples of the way Comenius passed from his interpretations of the "natural" to pedagogical analogues show how seductively plausible such thinking can be.

According to Comenius, Nature prepares the materials before she begins to give them form. This principle he transmutes into the pedagogical dictum that knowledge about the appearance of objects should precede the logical classification of them, and that an author's literary work should be studied before grammatical analysis of it is undertaken. But is any organic entity, in any stage of development, devoid of all form? Can any object or literary work be perceived or studied without some classification of it? It is not that form supervenes upon unformed matter, but rather than a more refined and articulated form takes the place of a less differentiated one.

Another natural principle, Comenius notes, is that Nature is not confused in its operations, but proceeds from one point to another. This, pedagogically interpreted, becomes the principle that the scholars shall be occupied with one unit of study at a time (Comenius, 1657, XVI; Keatinge, 1896, p. 271).

Or consider the principle that Nature carefully avoids obstacles and things likely to cause hurt. Aside from this doubtful interpretation of Nature, it is no small jump to the following pedagogical admonitions:

I. Receive no books but those suitable for their classes.
II. Books should be sources of wisdom, virtue, and piety.
III. Don't allow scholars to mix with bad companions in the school or in the vicinity of the school (Comenius, 1657, XVI; Keatinge, 1896, p. 278).

Understanding versus Imitation

From Comenius comes a strong plea for the understanding of what is learned as against mere memorization of verbal patterns, reflecting perhaps the influence of Francis Bacon's indictment of the literary "delicate" learning and his call for careful induction as a means to reliable and useful knowledge of the world. He urged that learners should not be set to any task until its nature had been thoroughly explained to them and rules for procedure given (Comenius, 1657, XVI; Keatinge, 1896, p. 272). All knowledge should be deduced from the unchanging principles of the subject in question, and no information should be imparted simply on bookish authority but instead it should be authorized by actual demonstration to the senses and intellect (Comenius, 1657, XVIII, 28; Keatinge, 1896, p. 302). Everything in science should be taught not only through the senses but also with reference to its true nature and origin, through its causes (Comenius, 1657, XX; Keatinge, 1896, pp. 341–342). But the examples Comenius gave of causal explanation resemble a genetic account of the phenomenon (an historical account of its development) rather than proofs of a causal hypothesis.

By a general notion of an object he seems to have meant a formal definition of it plus a listing of its parts. To "know" an object was to acquire information about the function and value of the several parts (Comenius, 1657, XX; Keatinge, 1896, pp. 342–343).

In spite of this intellectual and theoretical emphasis on the learning of concepts, rules, and principles, Comenius argued that we learn best by teaching others, hence we should let the pupil give the lesson to his fellows by repeating the words of the master. He further advised that the clever pupils be called up first (Comenius, 1657, XVIII, 44, 45; Keatinge, 1896, pp. 308–309). Apparently Comenius regarded the ability to repeat the words of the master as evidence of "understanding," for he remarked that frequent repetition will allow even the dullest to grasp it.

The suspicion mounts that Comenius' emphasis upon understanding, demonstration, and the like was really a plea for a change not in the method of teaching and learning, but rather in what was to be imitated and repeated. But is memorizing the law for the expansion of binomials, for example, intellectually a different task from memorizing the steps in explaining a binomial?

Comenius' emphasis on sense perception, his injunctions to correlate words with things, reading with writing, and amusement with serious study all seem to indicate that he was looking for a learning outcome that was not simple memorization. Yet when he justified the use of these approaches it was by the argument that they would facilitate the recall of specific answers to specific questions. Thus he advised that, as far as possible, instruction should be given through the senses so that it may be retained in the memory with less effort. It is useful, he said, for scholars to learn to write down in their notebooks everything they hear or read, for in this way imagination is enriched and memory assisted. The dictum: "Nothing should be learned by heart that has not been thoroughly grasped by the understanding," expresses succinctly Comenius' simultaneous loyalty to quite different intellectual processes and the learning outcomes corresponding to them (Comenius, 1657, XVII, 37, 41, 42; Keatinge, 1896, pp. 290–291).

Comenius argued for the use of the same method in the

teaching of science, arts, language, and morality, but the methods were essentially those used for skill formation or for perfecting desired responses to selected stimuli. With respect to the arts, the method was imitation of a model with correction on the spot by the teacher. Language teaching was, as has already been indicated, a matter of skill formation. Morality was achieved by teaching precepts and by conditioning. Because it is impossible to be so watchful that nothing evil can find entrance, stern discipline is necessary to keep evil tendencies in check (Comenius, 1657, XXIII, 7–8; Keatinge, 1896, pp. 364–365).

As to class control and motivation, Comenius seemed fully aware that they are not functions of the teacher alone. The parents, the civil authorities, the physical plant of the school, the method and content of instruction—all were vectors in the resultant climate of the school. The parents and authorities by pleasant and nonpunitive reinforcement of appropriate pupil behavior, the teacher by following the method of Nature, and the school by being a pleasant place with a garden and decorated walls could cooperate to make school and learning attractive (Comenius, 1657, XVII, 17–19; Keatinge, 1896, pp. 283–284).

Despite the doubtful deductions from the natural order, Comenius, when he played the role of a teacher and was dealing with the theory of teaching, was well ahead of his time. For example, the notion that schools begin their sessions at a uniform date and that children be admitted to them only at that time was not a common practice in his time; nor was the provision that each class have its own room and special teacher, or that children have textbooks that contained the work for each class.

Anticipating a problem that is still unsolved, Comenius frowned on homework, shrewdly guessing that it would probably be done indifferently. He did not perhaps anticipate a day when parents would be expected by their children to "help" with their homework. He wanted the children to tackle the harder subjects in the morning, and he believed in alternating work with relaxation. Simultaneous class instruction was urged by him more than a century and a half before the Brothers of the Christian schools used it and two centuries before Pestalozzi put it into effect (Eby & Arrowood, 1940, pp. 262–263). Although he counseled studying one thing at a time, he was shrewd enough psychologically to say:

> The sense of hearing should always be conjoined with that of sight, and the tongue should be trained in combination with the hand. The subjects that are taught should not merely be taught orally, and thus appeal to the ear alone, but should be pictorially illustrated and thus develop the imagination by the help of the eye . . . (Keatinge, 1896, p. 204).

Comenius' emphasis on the senses, although echoing what Aristotle and the medievals had said long before, was linked with the beginnings of revolt against the classical Humanistic curriculum and its values. There is talk now about useful knowledge, meaning thereby that "Whatever is taught should be taught as being of practical application in every-day life. That is to say, the pupil should understand that what he learns is not taken out of some Utopia or borrowed from Platonic ideas, but is one of the facts which surround us . . ." (Keatinge, 1896, p. 422).

This naturally led to the use of real things in the classroom; and if surrogates for real things be needed, they were to be in the form of charts, maps, drawings, diagrams, and similar perceptual approximations to the real things.

The Larger Vision

Comenius was a schoolman trying to systematize a dream. The dream was to educate and unify mankind, to bring it closer to God, and thus to its own perfection and happiness. The mission was to all the people and not merely to the well-born and powerful.

The key was provided by the natural order. The student was led from one bit of knowledge to another in their natural articulation. He was thus put in gear, so to speak, with the cosmic order itself. As his knowledge grew, it approximated the plenitude of Nature itself. And if by Nature one means the moral and psychical nature of man as well as the constitution of the psysical world, growth in moral perfection would proceed *pari passu* with growth in intellectual enlightenment.

Comenius had little choice, however, but to translate the dream into the pedagogical reality of teaching the Latin language. Within the limits of this enterprise, he exploited with great skill the opportunities for emphasizing content other than the content of the classical authors. Both the content and the method of empirical science as they were emerging left their traces on Comenius and his textbooks, as did the conviction that teaching was an art based on knowledge.

Chapter VIII

NATURE AND OBJECT LESSONS: PESTALOZZI

Johann Heinrich Pestalozzi (1746–1827) was one of those tragic figures whose failures are more understandable than his successes. His life and work illustrate the ambiguities that so often have surrounded school teaching. The difficulty of persuading the rich to carry out their professed admiration for schooling that does not directly pertain to the success of their own offspring, and of getting bureaucrats to carry out promises in the absence of massive political threats and reprisals is exemplified on virtually every page of Pestalozzi's biography. Even better does his life exemplify that combination of idealism, love of children, and enthusiasm so often found in the lives of great educational reformers.

Pestalozzi has been characterized as an emotionally volatile man, overinfluenced and overprotected by his mother and the nurse to whom his upbringing was consigned after his father died. In Pestalozzi's youth Zurich was a fine place to absorb the impacts of many movements. The local Collegium Carolinum boasted of such men as Professor J. J. Breitinger, a classical scholar, and J. J. Bodmer, teacher of Swiss history. The love of political freedom, the rationalism of the Enlightenment, the rapidly budding evil effects of industry on agricultural workers, the impulse to return to the pure simplicity of Nature before man had corrupted it, to be celebrated by Rousseau—all gave rise to a zeal for social reform. It is related that Pestalozzi and his friends slept on the bare ground and ate nothing but bread and vegetables to express their contempt for material well-being (DeGuimps, 1895, p. 10).

Like many other young men of modest means, Pestalozzi started out with the ministry in mind, but he never finished his theological studies. Instead, he turned to agriculture as a means of achieving happiness for himself and mankind. On a farm at Neuhof near Zurich he settled with his wife after their marriage in 1769. Despite elaborate plans and high enthusiasm, the agricultural venture failed. So he turned to writing, and in 1782 the famous *Leonard and Gertrude* was published. It gave Pestalozzi a reputation not so much for its pedagogical import, which was its major message, as for the sentiments it evoked. It dealt with the beneficent influence of a sweet, godly mother on children, despite a drunken father and the strictures of poverty.

An educational career became a clearer alternative to Pestalozzi after Johann Gottlieb Fichte, in urging the regeneration of the German nation through education, lauded his methods. Pestalozzi had conducted a school for the poor children of the neighborhood at Neuhof on the notion that the farm could be turned into a home factory of sorts, and that children could receive a practical industrial training and moral and intellectual training at the same time. It failed after a few years, but he had another chance at Stanz, where political developments made it feasible for him to establish a school for homeless children in 1798. This lasted for less than a year. His great opportunity came in Burgdorf (1800–1804), where he developed his philosophy and methods, and at Yverdon where he was forced to move his Institute in 1805 because the old castle he was using as a school was needed by the town authorities for other purposes. There after more than 20 years of work, Pestalozzi reached the peak of his success. Pupils came from all over Europe to live and learn in an idealized home and school.

In 1801 he published *How Gertrude Teaches Her Children,* and throughout his life he expounded his ideas in treatises, essays, and articles. His greatest influence, however, was exerted through the men and women who came to his institutes to observe and teach. Noted personages faced with educational problems came from other countries, especially from Prussia, which was reorganizing its school system. Scores of young people, including no less a figure than Friedrich Froebel, received their "teacher training" at Yverdon and later became educational leaders. Froebel was to remark later:

> Arithmetic was a very favourite study of mine; . . . But how astonished was I when, in my twenty-third year, I first went to Yverdon, and found I could not solve the questions being set to the scholars! This was one of the experiences which prepossesses me so keenly in favour of Pestalozzi's method of teaching . . . (Froebel, 1889, p. 20).

The distance between what was going on in Pestalozzi's school and the norm of expectation in the usual run of Swiss schools is revealed by the account Herman Krüsi (1775–1844), Pestalozzi's assistant for 16 years, gave of his own examination in qualifying for the post of schoolmaster in Gais toward the end of the eighteenth century.

Although his own schooling consisted of no more than "reading, learning by rote, and mechanical copying," and he had almost forgotten how to write, he applied for the job.

> The day of the examination came. An elder fellow-candidate was first called before the committee. To read a chapter in the New Testament and to write a few lines, occupied him a full quarter of an hour. My turn now came. The genealogical register, from Adam to Abraham, from the first book of Chronicles, was given to me to read. After this, chairman Schläpfer gave me an uncut quill, with a direction to write a few lines. "What shall I write?" I said. "Write the Lord's Prayer, or whatever you like," was the answer. As I had no knowledge of composition or spelling, it may be imagined how my writing looked. However, I was told to retire. After a short consideration, I was, to my wonder and pride, recalled into the room. Here chairman Schläpfer informed me that the whole committee were of the opinion that both candidates knew little; that the other was best in reading, and I in writing. '. . . Much attention was excited by the fact that my fellow-candidate, eight days afterward, took a situation as a policeman, in which he received three *gulden* a week, while the schoolmaster, who was obliged to furnish his own school-room, had to satisfy himself with two and a half.' (Krüsi, 1840, pp.

2–4; Cubberley, 1920b, pp. 373–374; translated in Barnard's *American Journal of Education*, 1858, V, 162–163).

Some Contrasts and Contradictions

Unlike Comenius, Pestalozzi was not tied to the teaching of Latin, because the poor whom he was determined to redeem through education no longer needed Latin for redemption. But like Comenius, his faith in education was boundless, and like Comenius, he was a hapless soul. Both suffered from the fact that their genius was more easily confounded by enthusiasm than clarified by logic. Both had visions which they were to share only with posterity; their contemporaries valued them for means—methods, materials, devices—rather than for ends.

This was especially true of Pestalozzi. His lifelong dream was to found and maintain a school for the children of the poor and to demonstrate that in this school these children would regain their dignity, humanity, and usefulness despite their poverty. But he never quite achieved this goal. Instead, his schools at Burgdorf and Yverdon became famous only when they were patronized by children from the middle and upper classes, that is, the exemplars of success. At Neuhof, where he lived for 30 years, the poor-school lasted only a few years, and at Stanz where he tried to educate homeless children and children of the poor, there was failure. He attributed the failure, and so did others, to his own impracticality; he seems to have been the world's worst school administrator. Nevertheless, the failure was not all due to his defects. The beneficiaries of the schools at Neuhof and Stanz, that is, the parents or relatives of the children, encouraged them to leave the school, especially after they had received clean clothes and food. His religious orthodoxy was under constant suspicion, and his political liberalism did not inspire confidence in the conservative members of the government and the business community.

He was a man in whom everything—the Enlightenment, the yearning for the return to Nature, the idealistic philosophy of the Germans, pietistic Christianity, the industrial revolution, social reform, and political fervor—was thoroughly mixed up and expressed in violent bursts of love for his fellow man and grandiose projects for educational establishments. This makes it difficult to characterize his theory, his practice, or his influence. Yet, if there is one point on which all commentators agree, it is that when he himself was in action among his pupils, something profound and important happened.

Seen in action, he presented, first of all, a father figure; an unkempt man whose unconcern for appearances was the despair of his wife and friends, but the figure of a father nevertheless. He loved the children, the villagers, servants, his assistants, and those whom he did not, at the moment, love, he forgave. The pupils' motivation to learning was clear and direct: it was love rather than fear. He managed to give emotional security to children who had known very little of it. Love *for* the child, he believed, would kindle love *in* the child: love of mother, of family, of man, and of God. The sense of duty and obligation would then follow naturally.

The loving heart was to be made effective in action by developing the powers of the hand and the head: the hand by training in manual skills and the tasks of home industry, the head by the clarification of experience through form, number, and language.

All this could be brought about if the general strategy of teaching aimed at releasing latent innate powers in children rather than that of forcing upon them the memorization of rules and facts remote from their powers and concerns. Little wonder that the stream of visitors to Yverdon and Burgdorf were amazed at the spirit and efficiency of the students. Again and again observers noted that the pupils "looked intelligent," presumably because they were behaving calmly and confidently with respect to the tasks presented to them. Not a little of this impression, however, was due to the performance of the children in mathematics where Joseph Schmid, one of Pestalozzi's controversial and contentious disciples, demonstrated the master's method brilliantly. Youngsters doing mathematics cheerfully are bound to give the impression of being unusually intelligent.

And this in itself brings one to the contrasts within Pestalozzi's institutions. On the one hand, there was the Method or what he sometimes referred to as Elementary Education (Silber, 1960, Chapter VI). He spoke of an elementary education of the head (intellectual), of the heart (moral), and of the hand (practical). Each had a starting point from which development could be guided by art (education) according to the laws of human nature.

As might be expected, Pestalozzi had some difficulty in deciding which of the three types of education is fundamental, because it turns out that each depends on the other two. But in the end it seemed to Pestalozzi that the moral and practical take priority over the intellectual. As is usual in theories of this sort, some kind of harmony constitutes the final objective, an outcome that is as difficult to quarrel with as it is to identify. So in visiting the Pestalozzi school, one saw and was impressed by the generally wholesome atmosphere of affection and cooperation among students and teachers. The freedom given to the pupil, the respect for his interests and capacities, the combination of work, study, and play, and the freedom of physical movement both astonished and excited the visitor, who probably had been put through a quite different regimen of schooling. Nor should it be forgotten that the school had a staff no more typical than its master. So do most experimental schools, and as a result, many a brilliant innovation in education trails off into mediocrity once it is transplanted from its experimental soil.

But there was another side to the school. Reading, writing, geography, and arithmetic, as well as music and drawing, were also taught. And while the general spirit of love and guidance pervaded all teaching at the Institute (or at least Pestalozzi assumed that it did), the visitor's attention would be caught by method in a narrower sense of the term. The general methodological principle of adjusting subject matter to capacity had to be translated into arithmetical concepts that could be taught to a pupil at a given time and the devices by which they could be taught. Whether the success of the school was the result of the general method, the special methods of the various subjects, or some happy combination of both is hard to decide. People came away with a determination to introduce one or both in their own schools, but since it was easier to imitate the procedures of teaching arithmetic than to be a Papa Pestalozzi, it was the special methods that survived the trauma of transplanting. For this reason, and because inspirational qualities are hard to verbalize, there is a temptation to downgrade the influence of Pestalozzi's general method. Like other educational reforms and insights, the Pestalozzian emphasis on the development of innate capacities, of teaching as elicitation, of growth as unfolding had a delayed but powerful effect, once they got into the vocabulary of schoolmen. Like the work of Rousseau, it made education pediocentric, although not egocentric as did later developments of the child-centered school.

Nature and ABC's

For Pestalozzi the term "Nature" meant, among other things, the nature of the physical world, in the sense that the world behaves according to unalterable laws. The pattern of physical nature Pestalozzi took pretty much from Newtonian mechanics, terrestrial and celestial. Human nature also has its unalterable laws, but they are the laws of development, and for education these were the crucial laws. Underlying all mental activity is *Anschauung*. *Anschauung*, usually translated as intuition, for Pestalozzi included virtually every cognitive operation from sense perception to the noetic apprehension of a concept. Intellectual development goes from obscure and confused experience to clear and definite cognition. It also moves from the simple to the complex, the concrete to the abstract, the particular to the universal (Silber, 1960, pp. 136 ff.).

Thus to follow Nature with respect to teaching reading, writing, and arithmetic meant beginning with the elements out of which these subjects are composed. But what is an element? There are times when an element is regarded by Pestalozzi as a part, e.g., the syllable is part of a word and the straight line part of the formation of the letter *A*. But at other times elements are conceived of as mental acts, such as form, number, and language, for these were the instruments by which gross perceptions were changed into clear concepts, i.e., into knowledge. *Number, form, and language* are, together, the elementary means of instruction, because the whole sum of the external properties of any object is comprised in its outline and its number, and is brought home to consciousness through language (Pestalozzi, 1894, p. 89).

For example, although all sense experience must possess some spatial form in order for us to perceive it at all, sensory experience becomes more manageable if it can be shaped by and broken down into simple forms such as the straight line, the triangle, and the square. The object becomes even more clear and distinct if one measures its formal shape. This is the element of number, and for Pestalozzi the simplest form of number is counting. Form and number reinforce each other, since the units of form are what we count. Hence it was important for young children to begin with real objects or things and thence progress to the more distinct notions. Note, if you please, that the square as a shape is, at the same time, both more abstract and more simple than, let us say, a pile of pebbles that has perhaps only a square-like shape. The pile of pebbles is a fine concrete introduction to the abstract operation of counting because it is both palpable and familiar, but note that it is not simpler than the abstract concept of numerical units. We shall return to this point.

The third of the elemental operations is language. Where should one begin here? Pestalozzi tried speech sounds and syllables as units. He wrote elaborate exercises which presumably led the child from simple sounds to their combination into words, phrases, and sentences. According to one commentator, the assistants compiled an *ABC of Measurement* and an *ABC of Form* to which Pestalozzi wrote the introduction. A projected *ABC of Language* never appeared although *Exercise Books* for the use of mothers were prepared in large editions (Silber, 1960, p. 144).

Physical education was also to have its own ABC of simple movements that were to be combined into more complex acts, for example, such generic movements as throwing, pulling, bending, turning. Just as gross perception becomes refined into distinct cognition by being reduced to its elements and then rebuilt, so does bodily control become perfected through appropriate sequences of elemental muscular actions.

In a Pestalozzian classroom one would see a multitude of real things. These were the concrete materials from which would be abstracted, by gradual induction and discrimination, clear ideas as to the properties of these objects and their modes of functioning. But one would also see, if the theory is to be believed, youngsters practicing curves and straight lines preparatory to writing, practicing the sounding of different combinations of letters into meaningless syllables prior to reading, practicing elementary muscle patterns prior to playing games, and the like. The modern observer would, of course, be immediately struck by this paradoxical combination of highly accepted and thoroughly rejected psychological principles of learning.

The Logical and the Psychological

When Pestalozzi spoke of the logical order of teaching, he meant simply that the order of instruction should conform to what we speak of today as the laws of learning. Educators have always been impressed by the fact that the physical development of the child seems to proceed ahead of the mental; that he moves and acts long before he speaks; that he speaks before he writes and reads; and that abstractions, especially abstract relationships, elude the child before a certain degree of maturation is achieved.

Pedagogically, this fact engenders the paradox that children learn informally, that is, without deliberate instruction, a wide variety of complex matters. They learn the geography of their neighborhood and village, the complicated syntax of their language, and all sorts of coordinations that are bafflingly complex when analyzed. Yet in verbalized form such materials are difficult for the child to learn. Hence, the educator has always been on the lookout for the secret of informal learnings so that it could be utilized in formal schooling. If the school could only teach arithmetic with the efficiency that a boy learns the batting averages of his favorite players! That a task is worked at harder and more steadily if it is related to a strong interest seemed reasonable enough, but what is there about interest that makes a task more learnable?

A clue to the mystery seemed to be that informally children deal with concrete, perceptible things in their surrounding and that these palpable objects are never wholly strange to them; they have been in the environment and have been perceived and handled as part of the normal activities of the child.

At Yverdon, geography was taught by direct observation of the surrounding valley, and children made relief maps of what they saw. This method is said to have inspired Carl Ritter's subsequent work in geography (Compayré, 1908a, pp. 90–91). Pestalozzi placed writing after drawing, and reading after oral exercise as evidence of his faith in the primacy of the concrete. Even in the moral field he wished the child to experience the sentiments of kindness and love before more verbalized formal instruction in moral precepts was given. How close this is to current advocacy of "guided discovery" and "unverbalized understanding" (Craig, 1956) is hard to estimate, because much of the current interest is with materials that resemble puzzles whose solutions are embedded in the "given" instances. With Pestalozzi the emphasis was on the directness and immediacy of experience.

This much of the methodology seems to follow directly from the primacy of the concrete and particular over the abstract and the general. When, however, Pestalozzi undertook to organize reading, writing, drawing, and other subjects for instruction, he operated on a somewhat different principle, namely, "Proceed from the simple to the complex."

In reading, for example, the materials were analyzed until the vowel sounds were reached as the basic elements. Points, angles, curves, and lines were the ABC's of drawing. He even hoped to reduce trade and physical training to elementary operations such as twisting, throwing, carrying, and the like. Presumably, by practicing on the elements, the pupil comes to be able to synthesize larger units. Or more accurately, learning the elements enabled him both to break up the unknown into the known and to combine the old elements into new combinations as needed.

In the moral life, the constitutive elements were the instinctive feelings or emotions that arose in the infant because of his relation to his mother—a sense of dependence, love, trust, and gratitude, developed as a response to her care and protection. Pedagogy was supposed to transfer these original emotions to mankind and then to God, according to Pestalozzi.

On the one hand, Pestalozzi regarded the concrete particular as easier to learn than the indirect (verbal), abstract, general symbol. On the other hand, he believed that simpler things are easier to learn than complexes. A letter is simpler than a word, and a word is simpler than a phrase. But a letter is also more abstract than a word in that it requires an act of abstraction to separate out letters or syllables from the concrete experiential whole used in spoken language. Was there a contradiction between concreteness and simplicity as guides to teaching?

By the logical order of a subject of study can be meant at least two things:

(a) A subject is logically organized if one can relate the statements within it by the rules of deduction or induction, e.g., mathematics or physics. In other words, the clues for relating the statements are in the logical properties of statements themselves.

(b) A subject is logically organized when its statements are arranged in some intelligible order: geography of the town, county, state, nation, continent, hemisphere, or letter, word, phrase, sentence, paragraph, and the like.

In the first sense of logical, the order is a property of the subject matter; in the second sense, the order is more or less external to the material, albeit intelligible. The analysis of materials into their elements is an example of the second kind of order. It is logical only in the sense that elements are logically prior to the complexes they make up, not that one element implies another. Moreover, this order may not correspond to the time sequence in which the materials came into the experience of the pupil. For example, in spoken language the child hears the word long before he hears the names of the letters; he experiences lines before geometrical points. The difficulty in learning elements arises not so much because elements are abstract or because they are logical, but rather because they happen to be less familiar than words or phrases.

Materials organized logically in the first sense, for example, as in mathematics or physics, may be difficult to learn because it takes a certain order of mental maturation to comprehend relations at certain levels of abstraction.

By the psychological approach Pestalozzi had in mind the notion of familiarity, on the one hand, and simplicity, on the other. The first led him to emphasize sense experience of real objects; the second impelled him to analyze all learning tasks into simple elements, not quite realizing, perhaps, as has been noted, that the familiarity gained by direct experience was partially cancelled out by the analytical approach.

Object Lessons

Gabriel Compayré (1908a, pp. 68–69) remarked that for Pestalozzi the outcome of instruction was primarily a clearer and fuller intuition of what was intellectually true, morally right and good, and practically efficient. Put differently, this could mean that the key to efficient learning was a set of images, concepts, or sensorimotor affective patterns that could serve as internal standards for the learner. Once the pupil had a model, it would guide the corrections of his trial responses. Pestalozzi realized that teaching should be concerned with helping the pupil acquire this criterion as rapidly as possible.

The concrete, the immediate, the particular, the familiar objects of experience are precisely what can furnish these vivid prototype intuitions. So important was immediacy to him that Pestalozzi said: "When I now look back and ask myself, what have I specially done for the very being of education? I find I have fixed the highest, supreme principle of instruction in the recognition of *sense impression as the absolute foundation of all knowledge*" (Pestalozzi, 1894, p. 200).

Along with the use of a real object, the object lesson called for a discussion that guided the class from sense impressions to the formal definition of the class of objects under study. It was, therefore, a method of presentation that encouraged concept formation by the learner. The formulation of rule, definition, and precept ended the lesson; it did not initiate it. This understandably made demands on teaching that conducting a recitation on previously assigned materials did not. It was a variation of the Socratic dialogue put into the service of teaching the common branches of schooling.

The object lesson and careful observation of objects provided a fine corrective for empty verbalism and mindless memorization, but where learning consists of an insight into a system of concepts bound together in a logical net, sensory discrimination has a limited usefulness. For example, watching the arcs described by a swinging pendulum, or noting changes in the water level of a vacuum flask inverted in a bowl of water as pressure is varied, does not disclose the explanatory principles. They do, however, give data for structuring the problem; they yield clues to the fruitful questions rather than to the answers. It should be remembered that, in Pestalozzi's time, science connoted careful inductions from sense observations more than rigorous conceptual systems, so object lessons seemed especially appropriate for the teaching of geography and nature in general.

The impact of this method on schooling in large part came from such texts as Colburn's *First Lessons in Arithmetic,* and through the work of Arnold Guyot (1807–1884) in geography and Lowell Mason (1792–1872) in music. The hosts of visitors to Pestalozzi's schools could copy down the results of his analysis of the various subjects into their ABC's and the sequence in which they were to be presented. They could also observe and duplicate such procedures as visiting the neighborhood and observing its geographical characteristics. They could note how object lessons were prepared and presented, how much time was given to each, and how learners were prompted to recite. Being a schoolmaster, Pestalozzi, like Comenius before him, did not scorn devices. He is credited with introducing the use of slates and pencils, letters of the alphabet fastened on cards, and even more important, simultaneous instruction of a whole class (Eby & Arrowood, 1940, p. 665). At a time when common education was about to expand rapidly in the New World, such methods were precisely what educational reformers could talk about and demonstrate to school officials and to prospective teachers.

Chapter IX

DIALECTICAL GARDENING: FROEBEL

Froebel wrote of himself:

> An intimate communion with Nature for more than
> thirty years . . . has taught me that plants, especially
> trees, are a mirror, or rather a symbol, of human life in
> its highest spiritual relations; and I think one of the
> grandest and deepest fore-feelings that have ever ema-
> nated from the human soul, is before us when we read,
> in the Holy Scriptures, of a tree of knowledge of good
> and evil. . . . I said my hazel buds gave me the clue of
> Ariadne. Many things grew clear to me: for instance, the
> earliest life and actions of our first parents in Paradise,
> and much connected therewith (Froebel, 1889, p. 12).

Once more we have to do with an eccentric, sensitive man
obsessed with the unfolding process of Nature in general and
of children in particular. Like Comenius and Pestalozzi he was
fascinated by the paradox that Nature in one sense fixed the
lines of this development, yet in another gave man the freedom
both to veer away from what is "natural" and to return to it
by education and will.

Born the son of a busy pastor in southern Germany in 1782,
Friedrich Wilhelm Froebel was deprived of his mother at an
early age. The unhappy youth turned to the fields, woods,
streams, and flowers in a lifelong search for inner peace and
unity. His early schooling was somewhat spotty, and he seemed
unable to decide upon a vocation. For a while he was appren-
ticed to a forester, and during one period he regarded himself
as an architect and surveyor.

In 1799 Froebel had occasion to visit his brother at the University of Jena and found the atmosphere there so stimulating that he remained to study. His Jena career ended with his spending nine weeks in the University prison for inability to pay his debts. In 1805 he set out to study architecture at Frankfurt but an invitation came to teach in the normal school. This apparently settled the problem of a vocational choice:

> The restlessness of youth, nay, that chance, rather, which has always lovingly guided me, threw me unexpectedly into relations with a man [Gruner] whose knowledge of mankind, and whose penetrating glance into my inner being turned me at our very first interview from the profession of an architect to that of a teacher and an educator, two spheres of work which had never previously occurred to me, still less had appeared to me as the future objects of my life. But the very first time I found myself before thirty or forty boys from nine to eleven years old, . . . I felt thoroughly at home. In fact, I perceived that I had at last found my long-missed life element (Froebel, 1889, p. 109).

No sooner had this occurred than he felt impelled to visit Pestalozzi's Institute at Yverdon, because he realized that his enthusiasm for teaching did not carry with it the knowledge and skill needed to do it well. He remained only a short time, but returned in 1808 with three young boys whom he had undertaken to tutor for Herr von Holzhausen in the suburbs of Frankfurt. He was enthusiastic about Pestalozzi, but not uncritical. For all the spiritual power of the Pestalozzian presence, the instruction, according to Froebel, was in many ways external, mechanical, and lacking in unity.

Still unsatisfied with his own cultural resources, he returned to university life, plunging into the study of the natural sciences, especially mineralogy, at Göttingen and Berlin. For a while it looked as if he could and would make an academic career for himself by teaching mineralogy, but his interest in education of the young was too strong. Froebel's search for unity in himself and in the world, his obsession with the notion of development, and the influence of Hegelian philosophy impelled him to begin a series of educational experiments with his Universal Educational Institute in Griesheim in 1816. The school was shifted to Keilhau the following year. Plans for a national educational institute at Helba foundered; another school was started at Wartensee and then transferred to Willisau.

And so it went, his schools running into debt and meeting opposition from the clergy at one place and creditors at another, yet attracting attention and a handful of devoted disciples who stuck with Froebel, despite hard times and the inflexibility of the master where educational doctrine and policy were concerned.

The turning point came in 1837 when the years of thought and experimentation issued in the establishment of the first kindergarten in Blankenburg. From then on, his enterprises for the training of kindergarten teachers prospered and his fame spread. His disciples carried the movement to Great Britain and the United States. After Froebel's death in 1852, societies for the study of the Froebelian methods sprang up, as did kindergartens, especially in the United States (Eby & Arrowood, 1940, p. 795).

The quest for a law of human development prominent in Comenius and Pestalozzi achieved theoretical articulateness in Froebel. His method of teaching, correspondingly, was more intimately tied to this notion than were those of his predecessors. Also significant was his extensive formal education in natural science and philosophy. For in Kant, Schelling, Fichte (whose lectures he attended), and Hegel, he had available a terminology and set of concepts that lent themselves to his special variant of German Absolute Idealism.

Because we are not primarily concerned with the rationale of educational aims, the complicated theoretical apparatus supporting the Froebelian outlook need not be detailed here. A word, however, must be said about a few of the key notions, or the methodology will fail to make any sense at all.

From his philosophical mentor, K.C.F. Krause, he took over the notion of organized unity, a unity in which any given thing is a whole in itself yet a part of a larger whole. The distinctive aspect of this relationship is not simply that of inclusiveness. It is rather that every individual thing exists *only* in its higher unity; the finger exists *only* in the hand and in that higher unity has a special function. Apart from hands there *are* no fingers. This notion, so fruitful in biology, was extended to the relations between an individual and the social order. In its name everything from artistic criticism to the totalitarian state has found justification. For one thing, in this view there is no end to the quest for meaning. The meaning of the finger is in the hand, but the meaning of the hand is in the arm, and that of the arm in the body, and that of the body in the totality of the environment which nourishes and sustains the body.

Where does one stop in this process short of the totality of all that is and all that can be thought of? We know nothing really until we know everything; no individual is truly important apart from his community and state; no subject of instruction is significant apart from the totality of the curriculum and life itself. Pedagogically, this sort of theory has the effect of leading the pupil on and on from one perch of significance to another more inclusive one. Furthermore, the individual pupil's significance swells as he is related to ever higher and more inclusive unities. All of these overtones reverberate in Froebel's theory of teaching.

Froebel was also devoted to the theory of recapitulation according to which cultural epochs are relived by each individual in his development from infancy to adulthood. He believed in the endless progress of man and the race to higher levels of development.

Finally, and 'perhaps most important for his methodology, is the notion that the developmental process is a swing between opposites toward a synthesis that unites them at a higher level— a process reminiscent of Hegel's dialectic, even though for Froebel it did not confine its operation to ideas. For Hegel any positive assertion, for example, "Man is a self," is a partial truth at best. How does a self acquire its uniqueness if not by opposing itself to the non-self, the other? The first sentence is called the thesis, the second is the antithesis. The mind oscillates between the two and cannot rest until both partial truths (moments) are transmuted (*aufgehoben*) in a third proposition, the synthesis. "Man is a citizen," for example, unites the separateness of the self and the other in the notion of the community.

The Method of Opposites

Opposition was regarded by Froebel as a necessary feature of all developmental process. Thus the inner *must* become outer or, as Hegel had said, the idea must manifest itself; the social *must* have an individual phase, and appearance *must* be an appearance of reality. Methodologically, this principle of opposites means that one looks for causes of behavior not in what resembles this behavior, but rather in what is radically different from it, a procedure not unfamiliar to psychoanalytic theory. "In good education, then, in genuine instruction, in true training, necessity should call forth freedom; law, self-determination; external compulsion, inner freedom; external hate, inner love" (Froebel, 1911, pp. 13–14).

It could be argued that Froebel formulated what is most distinctive in his method on the basis of this law of converse inference. Just as Karl Marx was to adapt the Hegelian dialectic of ideas as a formula for the class struggle, so Froebel used it to describe an approach to teaching.

All true education in training and instruction should, therefore, at every moment, in every demand and regulation, be simultaneously double-sided—giving and taking, uniting and dividing, prescribing and following, active and passive, positive yet giving scope, firm and yielding; and the pupil should be similarly conditioned: but between the two, between educator and pupil, between request and obedience, there should invisibly rule a third something, to which educator and pupil are equally subject. This third something is the *right*, the *best*, necessarily conditioned and expressed without arbitrariness in the circumstances. The calm recognition, the clear knowledge, and the serene, cheerful obedience to the rule of this third something is the particular feature that should be constantly and clearly manifest in the bearing and conduct of the educator and teacher, and often firmly and sternly emphasized by him. The child, the pupil, has a very keen feeling, a very clear apprehension, and rarely fails to distinguish, whether what the educator, the teacher, or the father says or requests is personal or arbitrary, or whether it is expressed by him as a general law and necessity (Froebel, 1911, pp. 14–15).

And he continues:

> This explains and justifies, too, the next requirement, and indicates, at the same time, the manner of its fulfillment: *The educator, the teacher, should make the individual and particular general, the general particular and individual and elucidate both in life; he should make the external internal, and the internal external, and indicate the necessary unit of both; he should consider the finite in the light of the infinite, and the infinite in the light of the finite, and harmonize both in life; he should see and perceive the divine essence in whatever is human, trace the nature of God to man, and seek to exhibit both within one another in life* (Froebel, 1911, pp. 15–16).

At first blush these passages seem to be a dialectical play on words, and even at a second glance such injunctions as " . . . he should consider the finite in the light of the infinite, and the infinite in the light of the finite, and harmonize both in life" hardly seem like prescriptions for a teaching routine. They do not describe behavior that is directly visible to the external observer. And yet they do refer to a teacher's attitude toward instruction, an attitude that is often indirectly but unmistakably revealed in a gesture, a tone of voice, and general demeanor.

All dialectical teaching utilizes indirect communication, even as did Socrates, its most remarkable exemplar. The use of opposites by the teacher prevents the pupil from resting too quickly in any result or becoming too easily satisfied with himself. Life situations are so complex that direct indicative language forms never describe them completely. Every proposition that asserts something about any real thing or event leaves out something; to be meaningful it has to define, that is, to limit itself. It is always relevant, therefore, when talking about existential situations to say: "On the other hand . . ." or "From another point of view . . . ."

Indeed, as Idealists have long asserted, there is no limit to the number of times one can say: "On the other hand . . ." because every new proposition is itself limited, and its opposite has to be invoked to complete it. The process makes it theoretically impossible to say anything that is really true without saying everything about everything. Thus in Hegel, for example, the unity which in the end validates all subordinate propositions is the Absolute in which the distinctions so unavoidable in ordinary human discourse are abolished and transmuted (*aufgehoben*). The method of opposites leads to a synthesis which combines the truth of the opposites. The pupil and teacher are unified in their willing subjection to the third higher entity—the right and the best, the ideal.

Unity

The ultimate unity is God. "All things have come from . . . the Divine Unity, in God Alone. . . ." "It is the destiny and life-work of all things to unfold their essence, hence their divine being, and therefore, the Divine Unity itself . . ." (Froebel, 1911, pp. 1–2).

Unification, connectedness, relationships were almost an obsession with Froebel. He looked for a unity in organic and inorganic life, and while studying mineralogy tried to unify the laws of crystal formation. As he said of himself:

> Chemistry fascinated me. The excellent teacher (Göttling) always demonstrated the true connection of the phenomena under consideration; and the theory of chemical affinity took strong hold upon me. . . .
> I was always highly delighted with his [Batsch's] expositions, for they suggested ideas to me which bore fruit both in my intelligence and in my emotional nature. Invariably, whenever I grasped the inter-connection and unity of phenomena, I felt the longings of my spirit and my soul were fulfilled. . . .
> My stay in Jena had taught me much; by no means so much as it ought to have taught me, but yet I had won for myself a standpoint, both subjective and objective. I could already perceive unity in diversity, the correlation of forces, the interconnection of all living things, life in matter, and the principles of physics and biology (Froebel, 1889, pp. 30, 31, 32).

The search for unity in diversity is also characteristic of aesthetic creativity. One criterion of aesthetic value is the degree to which the artist succeeds in unifying a wide diversity of elements so that every element is required by the whole and requires the whole for its own meaningfulness. Nothing is superfluous and nothing is dispensable. This resemblance to aesthetic activity is not accidental. The unity so dear to Idealism requires, among other unifications, the fusing of the True, the Good, and the Beautiful, the intellectual, the moral, and the aesthetic. In Froebel every act of teaching was simultaneously an intellectual, moral, and artistic enterprise, and its goal was a progressively evolving unity of experience for the learner. The harmonious development of heart, hand, and head so devoutly sought by Pestalozzi was given a philosophic foundation and a methodological form by Froebel.

Froebel's metaphysical system seems remote from the problems of teaching school, but his attitude toward the child in school might have been quite different had he not regarded each pupil as an unfolding of God's creative energy. Apart from this metaphysical posture, he would certainly not have dignified the games and prattle of the little ones by calling them revelations of the Divine nature. Nor would he have taken so seriously the symbolic import of "play" things, if they did not signify for him that every act of the child transcended both the childishness and the worldliness of the child's existence.

The metaphysical injunction that a third something, the right, should rule insensibly, a something to which educator and pupil are equally subject, suffuses the teacher-pupil relation with a spiritual glow that may explain why some people still insist that teaching, like preaching, is a "vocation" to which one is called by something higher than the need for earning a living.

Furthermore, the doctrine that man is a manifestation of the creative energy of God endows him with spontaneity and freedom. The notion of "negative" education, of permitting the child to express himself spontaneously, would not make much sense without such a hypothesis.

Finally, recapitulating the history of the race at various stages of child development would mean little without a theory of

evolutionary progress, and progress would make little sense without a criterion of value. The value criterion is the degree of
unification of all things in their relations to the unity of the
Divine energy.

Perhaps it is because Froebel's metaphysical position was so
strong and so elaborately detailed that his methodology was
never far from his theory—something that cannot always be said
for Comenius and Pestalozzi.

Mention has been made of Froebel's commitment to a form of
the recapitulation theory. This notion is important to education
and particularly to teaching for a number of reasons:

First, if there is any plausibility at all in the belief that the
child relives the various stages through which the race has
passed, then history provides us with a timetable for the "natural"
interests and activities of pupils. If, for example, nomadic hunting
is an early phase of racial development, then according to the
recapitulation theory, youngsters at a certain stage will feel
impelled to roam and hunt, and school teachers and curriculum
designers should take advantage of it. Educators have often
sought to define "stages" of development in some fixed sequence
but not always on the basis of the history of the race.

Second, if the recapitulation theory is correct, the literary
history of the culture can be scanned for materials peculiarly
appropriate for certain stages of development.

Third, if the theory can be relied upon, the school can exploit
the racial timetable by making sure that each stage prepares for
the next one. Failure on the part of the pupil can be diagnosed
as the result of irregular or improper passage through the various
stages.

Froebel outlined the stages of infancy, childhood, boyhood,
youth, and maturity, although he preferred to define each by
certain tendencies rather than by definite age limits:

> . . . in each child there is repeated at a later period the
> deed which marks the beginning of moral and human
> emancipation, of the dawn of reason—essentially the same
> deed that marked, and, inasmuch as the race was destined
> for freedom, must mark, the moral and human emancipa-
> tion, the dawn of reason in the race as a whole.

Every human being who is attentive to his own development may thus recognize and study in himself the history of the development of the race to the point it may have reached, or to any fixed point (Froebel, 1911, p. 41).

The Symbolic Object Lesson

In Froebel's hands the Pestalozzian object lesson was not just a focus for perceptual study of sense qualia, number, and shape. Nor was it primarily a trigger to set off conceptualization and verbalization. The object chosen for study was not just an object. It was selected because it had a formal quality that somehow suggested the Divine unity. Thus, the cube with its regular angularity and the ball with its regular curvature were symbolic of the way in which Nature develops by opposites. The cylinder mediates between the cube and the ball. How important geometrical properties were to Froebel is illustrated by the following:

> Now, since force develops and diffuses itself in all directions equally, freely, and unimpeded, its outward manifestation, its material resultant, is a *sphere*. For this reason the spherical or, in general, the round form is most commonly the first and the last form of things in nature. . . . Hence, too, the sphere resembles none of the other natural forms, and yet essentially contains the possibility and the law of all of them; it is, at the same time, formless and the most perfect form (Froebel, 1911, p. 168).

That drawing, clay-modeling, painting, coloring, singing, dancing, hearing dramatic stories, and the manipulation of blocks, patterns, and cardboard objects were activities suitable to preschool children, it took no Froebel to discover. But it did take a Froebel to endow these activities with the character of "occupations" that were to lead the child to closer identification with the Divine spirit and social unity. It also required a mystical imagination of no mean order to think of the cube and the ball as "gifts" of the Divine spirit, and to say that "play, is the highest phase of child development . . . *for it is a self-active representation of the inner representation of the inner from inner necessity and impulse*" (Froebel, 1911, pp. 54–55). It would be difficult to find a similar combination of metaphysical imagination and precision of method. History would lead us to expect that the routines of the kindergarten would remain, but that the metaphysical glow would fade from the eyes of Froebel's followers. That this did not always happen may indicate that the people attracted to Froebel's methods already had some of his metaphysical conviction: Mrs. Carl Schurz (who is said to have opened the first kindergarten in America in 1855), Elizabeth Peabody (who started the first English kindergarten in Boston in 1860), William T. Harris (who helped incorporate the kindergarten into the public school system in St. Louis in 1873), and Francis W. Parker, to mention a few of those who introduced the kindergarten to the United States.

No account of Froebel's method would be complete without mention of the famous circle. A large circle was painted on the floor of the room used as the kindergarten. The first exercise of the day required children and teacher to gather in the circle and to sing, pray, or play together. The circle has long been regarded as a "perfect" figure. Having neither a beginning nor end, it symbolizes continuity and regularity. No geometrical figure is more inimical to invidious distinctions. Froebel hoped that the children, by making the circle, would symbolically absorb its social and philosophical implications.

Kindergarten work is an unlikely career for anyone who does not love little children, and who is not impressed by the symbolic significance of everything they do. For taken at face value and by adult standards the child is indeed childish—clumsy, ignorant, and never too far from his nonhuman characteristics. Nor are children's potentialities great incentives to love them, because their future may be as pregnant with evil as with good. But when children are seen by a religious light in a transcendent relationship to a higher than human source, they can be treated with that rare blend of patience, love, and tutorial care so characteristic of the pioneer kindergarten teachers.

> . . . the school, as such, implies the presence of an intelligent consciousness which, as it were, hovers over and between the outer world and the scholar, which unites in itself the essence of both, holds the inner being of both, mediating between the two, imparting to them language

and mutual understanding. This consciousness is the *master* in this art, who is called *master* also because for *most* things he is to point out the unity of things. He is *schoolmaster* because it is his business to point out and render clear to himself and others the inner, spiritual nature of things (Froebel, 1911, p. 129).

To be sure, not all the results of Froebel's influence reflected the Idealistic romantic spirit of the kindergarten. The manual training movement—an extension of the Froebelian gifts and occupations—lost some of it when extended beyond the kindergarten. The same may perhaps be said of the speech, music, modeling, painting, and other motor forms of activity that were to become standard in elementary education. Other modes of justification, largely psychological, took the place of metaphysical romanticism.

Drawing, rhythmic activity, constructive manipulation of materials, and play—these are the activities that through Froebel's emphasis and systematic study have become the standard curriculum of pre-school training. Adults are often impatient to have the pre-school child begin reading, writing, and arithmetic. Or what is more often the case, schooling is thought to be useless for the very young, precisely because they are too young to study these subjects.

The radical import of the kindergarten is that it extended the period of formal schooling downward several years. This period was to be used to reinforce and enrich the stock of perceptions and feelings that would more efficiently induct the child into the adult social and intellectual world. Under the current stress on accelerating intellectual training, the pressure to use the kindergarten years for introduction to formal studies has increased. Whether or not the kindergarten should be used for this purpose is debatable. The modern home seems to be no more successful in preparing the emotions of the child for modern life than were the homes of a half century ago. If the mental hygienists are right in placing so much emphasis on the emotional and social factors at these early ages, Froebel was remarkably prescient in turning to the kindergarten for this purpose.

Of course, if one dismisses the elaborate and mystical theory of reality and divinity on which Froebel based his educational theory, the kindergarten loses its third dimension, and little else but childish play remains. For those innocent of this philosophy, the kindergarten and perhaps childhood itself must seem like a waste of time.

Froebel's metaphysical and quasi-mystical doctrines are a far cry from the language and spirit of modern child psychology. The question arises as to whether the respect for childhood, so ably championed by Rousseau and so thoroughly exploited by modern education, needs the Froebelian mystique for its sustenance. Will not the "facts" of emotional health and social efficiency convince parents and citizens that the kindergarten or its equivalent is worthy of their support?

Modern psychology has given a solid and nonsentimental basis for mental hygiene and careful attention to child development, but unless a culture is entranced by the potentiality of childhood and passionately devoted to its realization, the commitment to the long nurture of the young will be prudential at best. Once the "cosmic" dimension of childhood is dropped, the life and activities of the child degenerate either into means to be manipulated for the benefit of adults or into a necessary but unfortunate marking of time.

Chapter X

INSTRUCTION AS CONSTRUCTION: HERBART

Johann Friedrich Herbart (1776–1841) was an "educationist" in what ever honorific connotation that term retains. He had a primary, not an incidental, interest in pedagogy. He wrote extensively in the field of professional education, established an experimental school, and systematically related his educational theories to his work in metaphysics, ethics, and psychology. Finally, he was a university professor whose writings had made his name and teaching method virtually synonymous by the end of the nineteenth century. His own lectures attracted throngs of students at Königsberg, where he took over the most renowned chair in philosophy, that of Immanuel Kant, in 1809.[1]

Herbart's teaching method has been divided into steps. His followers transformed Herbart's notions of clearness, association, systematization, and method into the steps of (a) Preparation, (b) Presentation, (c) Association, (d) Systematization, and (e) Application.

As names for teaching procedures, these steps presented little that was new; formulations of them could be found from Isocrates on. The steps interest us because of the conceptual framework used to justify them and because of the specific ways they were to be used in teaching organized bodies of subject matter. Any method that lists "steps" will cause teachers and prospective teachers to take out their notebooks.

Psychologically, the Herbartian approach is important because

---

[1] It is recounted that he began the manuscript for his *Hauptpunkte der Logic* one midday and delivered it to the printers the next noon (Herbart, 1893, p. 16).

it makes cognition the basic psychological activity, with feeling and willing derivative from cognition. Abandoning innate capacities and powers, Herbart believed that he could build up all human experience out of presentations (*Vorstellungen*) that enter experience via the nervous system. Out of the impressions of sense, pain, and pleasure come derived presentations. Those presentations which reflect the idea or thing that caused them, by comparison, abstraction, and generalization, develop into concepts (indirect sensuous presentations). The child in school has already acquired stocks of presentations from experience and from intercourse with others. The former, through instruction, eventuates in knowledge, the latter in sympathy (Herbart, 1893, pp. 33–34).

Accordingly Herbart remarks:

> Capacity for culture then, depends not on a relation between several primordially distinct capacities of the soul, but on a relationship amongst each other of presentations already acquired, and again between them and the physical organization. In both respects the pupil will need careful observation (Herbart, 1898, p. 114).

These basic elementary ideas have a power or dynamism of their own that drives them to achieve consciousness. They are metaphysical "reals" that strive to persist. They compete with other ideas or idea clusters for a place in the field of awareness. When driven out of consciousness, they remain latent in the unconscious striving always to return. In this campaign they can unite with other congruous ideas and summate their separate powers. Congruity among ideas is felt as pleasant; conflict between them as pain. Choice is determined by the nature of the idea clusters dominating the field of consciousness at any given moment.

Pedagogically, Herbart's system is important because it makes instruction a controllable process of building idea clusters that constitute the apperceptive mass. Each idea cluster can be thought of as carrying a power index, or exponent, so that theoretically, at least, one might have a calculus of probabilities as to what choices the individual will make, given the power values of his ideational components. In a way, Herbart translated the Socratic "Virtue is knowledge" formula into psychological and pedagogical terms. Inasmuch as everything depends on the specific input of ideational material, teaching can be rationalized and methodized.

Turning now to the steps of teaching method, we shall try to indicate how each one identified an important phase in any teaching method and how it operated in Herbartian pedagogy.

Preparation

Preparation for the teaching act has two aspects, which may be called the motivational and the cognitive. Motivational preparation refers to procedures instituted to arouse and maintain attention of the learner in the learning task. Some motivating devices are extrinsic to the nature of the learning task, e.g., commands, demands, threats, or sudden loud noises. Another type of motivational strategy takes advantage of interests already developed in the learner. For example, knowing that seven-year-old boys are deeply interested in gunfighters and weapons of all sorts, one can secure attention by showing a rusty flintlock to the class. While the first type of motivating is wholly extrinsic to the learning task, exploiting an existing interest may or may not be. The learning task in the example given above might well be related to weapons, but it might also be a dramatic introduction to a lesson on oxidation. Herbartians used both the extrinsic and the more intrinsic types of motivational preparation. Strict discipline (government) was used to command attention, but use of the recapitulation theory (cf. Chapter IX) enabled them to exploit certain interests that children at various stages of development were supposed to have as they re-enacted the development of the race. In any event, Herbart advised that "with all instruction which cannot at first be given without some constraint, the chief thing is to make the pupil aware of his own progress as soon as possible" (Herbart, 1898, p. 143).

Herbart believed that the simple social relationships most likely to impress children were to be found in the lives and activities of earlier peoples as expressed in the literature of those people, e.g., the *Iliad* and the *Odyssey* of the Greeks. His followers worked out in great detail the cultural materials appropriate for various age levels, utilizing materials progressing from Mother Goose, to the Old Testament, to epic literature of the Greeks, to the New Testament, to modern literature (Eby & Arrowood, 1940, p. 780).

On the cognitive side, preparation involves "the summoning up of a mental escort into the presence of the newcomer to welcome and introduce him" (Compayré, 1908b, p. 36). Preparation can take the form of the recall of materials similar to those in the learning task, analogous or opposite to it, antecedent to it, a result of it, or in some other way relevant to the learning of it. So the apperceiving presentations have to be inventoried and brought clearly into consciousness. If the old presentations are too few, too confused, or not in the right order to assimilate the new material, the teacher has to make them so.

Part of this preparation the teacher does alone before the class meeting. He makes a rough outline of what he can expect to find in the pupils' arsenal of experience. The second part is an interrogation of the class in which the pupils are encouraged to speak freely of everything that in any way relates to the topic. Out of this the teacher selects for summarizing and stress only the most essential notions, those crucial for apperceiving the new material (Felkin & Felkin, 1898, pp. 108–110).

Naturally, the good teacher is looking for a preparatory procedure that will be both motivationally and cognitively effective. The conventional subject-matter curriculum was hard to motivate intrinsically, i.e., by devices that are intrinsically related to the learning task, while "felt" needs or native interests may not point toward learning tasks that fit into the conventional subjects.

Herbart solved the problem by arguing that the very act of apperception is satisfying in itself and consequently arouses a desire to continue the process, especially if it proceeds with ease. Further, each idea cluster as it developed became "an interest" with power to invade consciousness. Hence, many-sided interest was for Herbart more than a phrase connoting all-round development. It was rather a design for instruction so that the empirical, speculative, aesthetic, sympathetic, social, and religious aspects of experience would all receive their due and reinforce each other (Herbart, 1898, pp. 147–148).

Presentation

Presentation has for its objective a clear awareness of whatever is to be apperceived as a single object or unit, that is, a story, a specimen, an experiment, and the like. The emphasis placed on the scrutiny of and absorption in an object apart from all other objects is, of course, witness to the continuation of the belief in the object lesson and the virtues of observation.

Herbart did not idolatrize sense perception as did some of the followers of Pestalozzi. Nevertheless, vividness helped apperception, and clarity of perception helped even more. Presentation was not confined to sense perception; all sorts of verbalizing were encouraged. Herbart realized that the real foe of understanding was not language, but rather unorganized aggregates within the experience of the learner, or, more accurately, the villain was the discrepancy between the organizing principle of the pupil and that of the subject matter being taught to him. This is, once more, the problem of the logical and psychological order in teaching; hence, the great care enjoined by Herbart in both preparation and presentation.

In connection with presentation Herbart spoke of the alternation of concentration (*Vertiefung*) and reflection (*Besinnung*) as a kind of mental respiration (Herbart, 1893, p. 126n). Pedagogically, this respiration was sustained by having the pupil attend to the new material as an element with its own characteristics and then allowing the several elements within the new material to intermingle and fuse in as many ways as possible.

Association and Systematization

Properly carried out, preparation and association complete the apperception of a single object or unit of instruction: a poem, an event in history, a geometrical principle. The next step, called association, was designed to enable the student to attain concepts by comparisons and contrasts among instances of the phenomenon being studied. Systematization grouped the information and principles elicited in the lesson, e.g., the various forms of speech would be one such principle of grouping, parts of the body might be another. Or as one commentator put it, "This systematic order is again the parallel to the well-arranged library in which a book can be instantly found" (Felkin & Felkin, 1898, p. 115).

Perhaps the most interesting aspect of the Herbartian emphasis on association and systematization is the fact that in the history of pedagogical theory there has always lurked a counter-emphasis. Classification and orderly hierarchies of concepts, or of anything else for that matter, irked spirits who believed that life could not be confined to pigeonholes and systems. Above all, they rebelled against the notion that the mind of the young child was or should be developed into such a set of pigeonholes. In romantic periods of civilization this rebellion has been especially strong, and the notion of development as a kind of organic growth has become popular. Sometimes (as in the case of Froebel) this growth was thought to be directed by inner principle; sometimes (as in the case of romantic literature and music), the growth was expressed by increased intensity of feeling.

Disagreeing with Fichte, his teacher, and other German Idealists, Herbart rejected the idea that reality is one unified whole from which all partiality and abstractness is removed (*aufgehoben*) in the Absolute. To be real is to be a self-sustained unity, but there can be many such unities, i.e., a plurality of reals. Each human soul, each idea was such a reality with its own character and its own power for sustaining itself in existence. Each real could be related to others. The relations do not change the nature of the things being related. On the contrary, the nature of the ideas, to a large extent, determines which will best combine with others.

Teaching, therefore, is the systematic exploration of the most fruitful way of clustering the elements of experience both for their storage and for their retrieval. Some schemes of classification or clustering can handle large amounts of information efficiently; others cannot. In our culture the intellectual disciplines provide our best models of classificatory efficiency, and it is to them that we turn for the logical order of both subject matter and human thinking.

There are, to be sure, other ways of organizing new experience—in terms of our interests, in terms of their emotional intensity, in terms of our social roles, in terms of our ideals and hopes. Some of these latter schemes of clustering experience seem more spontaneous, more natural, more lifelike than the logical classification. Froebel was certainly more romantic than Herbart in this respect and so was Pestalozzi, although when it came to teaching certain subjects, the latter was more analytical than romantic (Chapter VIII).

Hence, although the systematization and association steps lead to what many have regarded as desirable outcomes of schooling, the Herbartian methodology has been criticized as mechanical and as giving the teacher too much control over the mind of the pupil. The appearance of the Freudian analysis of experience, together with the Darwinian description of the way in which living things acquire their survival traits, shifted the emphasis to nonlogical modes of organizing experience. If our lives are shaped by the demands of the libido and natural selection, then learning as well as all other modes of experience will take its cue from them rather than from logic and theoretical systems.

Application

In the last phase, called philosophizing, methodizing, or application, exercises are given to the pupil to test the adequacy of the previous steps. The crit rion is the firmness with which the new learning has been incorporated into the apperceptive mass, the number of interest clusters with which it has made connection, and the readiness with which it can be expected to function in future learning. The series of ideas may be repeated forwards or backwards from different starting points; or the pupil may be asked to give an instance to illustrate a generalization, or to cite the generalization that a given case illustrates. Problems of various sorts are also means of teaching application.

In discussing the general structure of method, reference was made to the distinction between the evaluation trial and the practice trial (Chapter I). In the practice trial, teacher and pupil cooperate to correct errors or to reinforce the right performance. In the evaluation trial, help from the teacher is withdrawn and the pupil is asked to recite, write an examination, solve a problem, or imitate a model.

These "payoff" trials are judged by the teacher and sometimes marked or graded. Such judgment and the trial itself are part of the teaching process in a sense that a "life" trial is not. As Herbart said: "Even superficial experience teaches us that the results of an examination are valid only for the day when it is held . . ." (*Brief Encyclopaedia*, sec. 105; Ulich, 1954, p. 510).

The application of learning to materials not practiced is a test trial *par excellence*, especially as a test of generalizations achieved in the previous step. An apt application not only tests the learning, but improves it, because every successful application or even intelligent failure to apply a generalization enlarges or reorganizes the apperceptive mass.

As to life tests, Herbart, as has been noted, placed his faith in the belief that certain idea clusters would become sufficiently powerful to displace their rivals in the field of consciousness. Thus, the idea cluster representing us as happy with the loot from a bank robbery, if no hindering representation intervenes, and if accompanied by the belief that the bank robbery can be brought off, will result automatically in a try at bank robbery. Everything depends at this juncture on whether another idea cluster (an idea cluster, let us say, which represents us as jail-birds in disgrace and includes a strong belief in the probability of being caught) displaces the earlier cluster in consciousness. And this intervening cluster will appear only if it has been built into the experience of the learner in such a way that it has the power at critical points to forge into consciousness.

For this purpose Herbart favored materials from history and literature, .because they offered such a rich and vivid source of ideas about moral situations, alternative solutions, and their consequences.

The mechanical aspects of the formal steps tend to obscure

the fact that Herbart hoped through them to achieve a flexible use of knowledge, from what he called the "circle of thought."

"Courage," he said, "then, will be sustained by the certainty of the *inner* performance, and rightly so, for the external impediments which unexpectedly appear to the foresight of a careful intelligence, can terrify him but little who knows that, with altered circumstances, he can at once evolve new plans" (Herbart, 1898, p. 213).

It should be clear, even from this very brief description of the Herbartian steps and the theory underlying them, that systematic control of the instructional process has taken the place of the mystical enthusiasm about inner development so characteristic of Comenius, Pestalozzi, and Froebel. Perhaps the fact that Herbart's life was more conventional and less tragic than those of the others we have named, helps to account for the difference in mood. He was born of a good family in northwest Germany and received a good education at all levels. He did well in school and liked it; the others, by and large, were not happy with their formal schooling. Whereas the scholarship and theoretical caliber of Comenius, Pestalozzi, and Froebel were not the bases for their claim to greatness, Herbart's was.

In its struggle for professional status, school teaching has relied more on the personal greatness of a Pestalozzi or a Froebel than on the scholarship of a Herbart. The dedication and greatness of soul of the enthusiast stir a culture to reform its educational activity, an achievement beside which professionalization is a low-keyed goal. Yet it is professionalization that makes the visions of the great reformers effective, and for professionalization, scholarship and discipline count as much if not more than dedication.

In 1797 Herbart decided to become a tutor to the three sons of a Swiss official. During the three years in which they were in his care, he had a chance to observe carefully and precisely the relation between instruction and learning. Between 1802 and 1809 he wrote his chief works on education (Eby & Arrowood, 1940, p. 759), including his *General Pedagogy: Essentials of Metaphysics and Essentials of Logic* in 1806. Later came the works on philosophy and psychology.

INSTRUCTION AS CONSTRUCTION

According to his translators, Herbart's educational prescriptions have three aspects: government, instruction, and discipline (Felkin & Felkin, 1898, introduction).

Government has as its object the creation of order and hence the task of keeping the pupil within bounds. To bring this about, the teacher can use occupation (keeping the children busy), supervision, and threats, with or without punishment. Inasmuch as discipline is discussed separately, government presumably refers to class control rather than to individual pupil control. Government, one might say, consists of the rules that enable teachers and pupils to make judgments about what is permitted and what is forbidden in the classroom.

Discipline, on the other hand, seems to refer to direct and indirect attempts to influence the character of the pupils. By character is meant the reliable disposition to choose and act out of knowledge and on the basis of moral principle. Herbart was no more optimistic about the power of ordinary experience to provide moral principles than about its power to provide scientific ones.

Indirectly, character was to be formed by instruction that would enable the pupil to judge and choose in accordance with knowledge. Directly, character was to be formed by the praise and blame which the teacher affixed to the actions of the pupil. The teacher was to appraise both the material rightness of the act (producing the appropriate consequences) and the formal rightness of the act (acting from the right motive). Self-discipline or mature character is achieved when the person's motives are controlled by his self-concept and when his actions are shaped by knowledge. The first control takes care of the right intent; the second of the right consequences.

Character education brings together the factors of cognition and feeling and focuses attention on the concept of interest that combines them so well. Herbart and Dewey both sensed the strategic importance of this concept in educational theory, and it may be appropriate to compare Herbart's notion of the circle of interest with the theory of interest made famous by John Dewey (1895, p. 29) and William H. Kilpatrick.

In one sense, Herbart's exhortation to cultivate many objects of interest, or to study a given object in numerous aspects, points to interest for the sake of interest. This emphasis is accentuated when the distinction is drawn between interest and desire. Interest, according to Herbart, has to do with the present, presumably with the characteristics and relations of the object being studied. Interest is the attention that a *desire to know* compels, and it is intellectual. Desire in the ordinary sense of the word points to the *future* and envisages the possession of the object desired; desire is the instigator to overt action. The desire to know, if we take this distinction seriously, is not a desire to act in order to possess some material or psychological pleasure. It is no more than an impulse to perceive, intuit, or understand the object. In Herbart's terms such understanding is the apperception of the object, the comprehension of it in its relatedness to the whole of one's experience, including its volitional ingredients.

The distinction, if tenable, is important for teaching method. If interest is the result of action and action alone (as Dewey seems to hold), then action is the crux of the method for getting and maintaining the interest of the class. On the other hand, if the pupil can be moved by a purely intellectual interest, that is, by a desire to know, the strategy for motivation need not be tied to action. The curricular and methodological developments since World War II, it would seem, have favored the Herbartian view of interest. Nevertheless, no one can doubt that action implies involvement and interest; action is a sufficient condition of interest, but if we are to believe Herbart, not a necessary condition.

The influence of Herbart on pedagogy was enormous in this country as well as in Germany. Charles DeGarmo, C. C. Van Liew, Charles McMurry, and his brother Frank McMurry brought back from Germany during the last decades of the nineteenth century the principles of Herbartian psychology. A National Herbartian Society was founded in 1892, and became the National Society for the Study of Education in 1902.

In evaluating the Herbartian style of teaching, one can only repeat comments made on some of the previous exemplars of teaching method. The method is rarely much better than the person using it, yet the personal factor is not quite of the same importance in all the methods. Without "Papa" Pestalozzi, without Froebel, without Socrates, their respective methods limp and on occasion seem silly. The Herbartian steps, on the other hand, require erudition and skill on the part of the instructor, but the dependence on personality is less crucial. A competent teacher trained in the Herbartian method and equipped with good general education may not bring off a brilliant lesson day after day. Nevertheless, if he follows the steps intelligently, it is rather difficult for him to come up with a poor one.

Although character is the ultimate goal of schooling for Herbart, it is his reliance on formal instruction in intellectual content to achieve character that is distinctive of his methodology. He has been criticized for overemphasizing the role of the instructor in schooling, but it remains true that the instructional phase of education is the one most directly and surely under the control of the school. Accordingly, study and research of the instructional transaction is the "basic" research of education. If the Sophists were the remote ancestors of the educationists, Herbart was the direct progenitor of education as a field for scholarship and professional study.

Chapter XI

LEARNING AS WHOLEHEARTED DOING: KILPATRICK

The genius of the American social experiment was expressed in shaping a way of life for men who wanted to control their own land, their own business, and their own decisions in matters public and private. The English idea of a free citizenry, extended by the American Revolution to all members of the body politic, became the key notion in that complex of ideas and feelings we call democracy.

Where matters were a concern of the community, the rights of the individual were to be shaped to the common good, but even in such circumstances the individual was given the right to participate in deciding what the common good was to be. Freedom from a tyrannical government, freedom from the inherited privileges and equalities of a fixed class system, and freedom from the demands of an established church were to be the ingredients of the new social order.

This ideal was especially attractive because in a new land with open frontiers the notion of each man on his own land or conducting his own business as he saw fit had a great deal of initial plausibility. With no system of nobility and no established church, one could live in communities made up of one's peers. Each man in such a small community could be free and yet obedient to the common good. The community told everyone— often without words—what was right and what was wrong, but the likemindedness and likeheartedness of the group were so great that community pressure was rarely felt as alien or external. For the most part the demands of the community and the dictate of one's own sense of decency were identical. The rare exceptions furnished the stuff out of which scandals and tragic novels were made.

When conflicts did arise, they took place within a common framework of values: Differences arose about the meaning of the common good in a particular instance or about the means for securing it. By discussion and persuasion, by bringing the intellectual resources of the group to bear on the problem, a solution could be found that all or most of the group could live with. Parliamentary devices were used to register the decision once debate was over.

During the latter half of the nineteenth century, hordes of immigrants came to America, and the homogeneity of feeling in many communities, especially urban ones, was destroyed. People accustomed to the class systems and autocratic governments of the old country had to *learn* to feel the urgency of the democratic spirit. Indeed, many of them did not realize that participation in decisions affecting even their private welfare—not to speak of the common good—was theirs as a right and not merely as a gracious grant of privilege by the monarch. Community likemindedness no longer served as unquestioned frames of judgment, because it was no longer communal. How to assimilate the foreigner to the American way of feeling and acting, accordingly, became the great challenge to the schools in the late nineteenth and early twentieth century.

Another factor was also disrupting the unity of the small community in America. This was the spread of the industrial revolution to these shores and the growth of cities that accompanied it. Specialization in vocation and the dependence of technology on science created fields of knowledge that were not the common possession of all. The day when a boy learned the technology of the culture by doing the chores around the house and farm was gone. More and more of the concepts crucial to the culture were stored in esoteric disciplines and could not be picked up in the ordinary processes of day-to-day living. Less and less of what was most important in the culture was, therefore, a matter of common knowledge. Neither in knowledge nor feeling did the urbanized mechanized city of the twentieth century enjoy the homogeneity of the earlier and smaller American community.

It is therefore not surprising that educational theorists saw the problem of the school in the early part of the century as a restoration of the face-to-face controls of the small, semi-rural community. Because they could not return American modes of living to the small village or town, it seemed reasonable for them to regard the school as the instrument by which, as John Dewey put it, the school could provide the city with a simplified, balanced, and purified environment, that is, an ideal community (Dewey, 1916, pp. 22–26).

In such a school, the life of the nonschool community would be simulated. In the world outside of the school, community is achieved through sharing the tasks of living. To work together, people must share both the understanding of the task and their attitudes toward it. Outside the school, people learn by doing or by living; they either learn or perish, and because so much depends on learning, the participants are highly motivated, that is, they are *inter-esse*, in the middle of things, and therefore, concerned about the outcome. The school as the ideal community would also exhibit these ways of living and learning.

How many times a teacher has wished that children in school would work as devotedly on their lessons as they do on collecting frogs or stamps, or on building a shack or boat! Suppose that the school took its nose out of lessons and books and became a place where young people collected frogs, built boats, and did other things that in their age and station really mattered? Obviously, the problem of motivation would be solved and with it more than half of the other problems of schoolkeeping.

If one puts together all the factors listed above—the need for a purified, balanced, and simplified community, and the need for motivating children to learn to share their cognitions and feelings about the common good—then the next step seems almost inevitable. An activity curriculum replaces the traditional curriculum of symbolic skills, facts, rules; overt activities replace merely verbal ones.

Perhaps one more factor ought to be introduced to round out the reasons for the profound appeal that this development had for schoolmen from the twenties onward. John Dewey was a philosopher as well as a philosopher of education. It seemed to him that man had made relatively little progress in moral and social life in comparison with his progress in science and technology (Dewey, 1920, 1929). He blamed this on the classic theories of knowledge and reality. In regard to the theory of reality, he charged that the ancients presupposed reality to have been fixed and unchanging, organized on principles that were eternal and emanating from a super-sensible source of Perfection. To know, therefore, was to apprehend these principles. To know was to capture the essences of the individual things of the world by defining them in terms of their species and genus, that is, to locate them unambiguously in the fixed pigeonholes of the world's structure.

Such a view of the world, Dewey argued, discouraged and belittled change in general, but especially change in social arrangements that also were supposed to have been ordained as the best possible arrangements in the best of all possible worlds. Suppose, Dewey suggested, the world is not fixed and finished; suppose no eternal principles of Perfection control it; suppose man can change the social reality as he changes his physical environment by the employment of scientific method.

These suppositions gain support from the way the best knowledge we have—science—is achieved. How then does modern science reach warranted assertions? Modern science, according to Dewey, cares little about the metaphysical natures of things and much about the laws describing their behavior. What a thing will do is more important for control than what it is. Or, to put it another way, what a thing is is revealed in what it does. Now science proceeds as follows: It begins with a predicament, a felt difficulty, of which one becomes conscious only when ordinary action is impeded. When this occurs, as when one's automobile sputters to an unexpected stop, one is forced to become fully conscious of the situation.

The next step is to convert the predicament into a problem. Sometimes we do not make this conversion. By trial and error, by poking under the hood, rattling the starter, pulling a wire here and pushing a rod there, the car is persuaded to start. But when such haphazard measures are inadequate, one is forced to ask: "What is the difficulty here?" "Just what is preventing the car from running?"

Closer examination of the situation follows, and during the examination, one's knowledge about motor cars is put to use. The more one knows about automobile engines, the more likely he is to be able to note candidates for the role of the villain. The less one knows about motor cars, the more quickly the scrutiny of the situation will be reduced to a mere staring, and unless something obvious such as gushing liquid, flames, or a dead pigeon is found under the hood, the novice will get nowhere. He will, instead, change his problem from "What is preventing this automobile from running?" to "Where and how can I summon a service man?"

If, however, something does come of the scrutiny, we frame hypotheses as to the cause of the motor failure. We hypothesize that it might be the fuel line or the lack of fuel or fuel pump or the ignition, or . . . .

Calling once more upon our fund of generalizations about automobiles, we formulate tests for these hypotheses. The one about the fuel tank is simple. The others are somewhat more intricate, but with a picture of the whole system in the mind, it is possible to set up "If . . . then" statements as tests. If the fuel line is broken, there ought to be a leak somewhere. If the battery is dead, the lights will not go on or else will shine very dimly. The important point is to think up tests that one can apply—to think up things to do that will either verify or falsify the guesses.

The heart of modern scientific method, Dewey believed, was the way it combined ideation (concepts) with overt muscular acts. An idea or a proposition was true if the experiments one designed to test it came out as predicted. Thinking, the best kind of thinking, Dewey concluded, included an overt doing. The act of thought began with a problem or a problematic situation and ended with an action that converted it into a clear situation, one in which the interrupted action could proceed on its prosperous way (Dewey, 1910).

Dewey's *How We Think* had a wide circulation among professional school people. It brought to professional educators a sophisticated theory of knowledge in popular form. It was only natural, one must repeat, that if the act of thought was as Dewey described it, the act of learning could and should have the same form. We learn by thinking, but thinking involves doings as its first and last *termini*. The first doing is the predicament, the interrupted action. The last doing is the testing act which warrants our assertions and verifies our hypotheses. If this is how we learn, then this is also how we teach. In short, the teacher sees to it that there are predicaments or better still, he guides his pupils to carry out the steps of the act of thought whenever he finds himself in a predicament. What the scientist does in his study and laboratory with refined apparatus and concepts, everyone can do in ordinary problems of life, and the school can do no better than to habituate the young into attacking its predicaments in this fashion.

Although John Dewey was the philosophical ancestor of the activity curriculum and the problem-solving style of teaching, the man who probably had most to do with bringing this method of teaching into the American school system was William H. Kilpatrick (1871–   ).

Born in White Plains, Georgia, a small agricultural town, Kilpatrick was not a turbulent spirit from whom one might expect revolts against tradition. By his own description he was a good boy, kept all the regulations, and was orderly in all his habits. He was even good in school. Nor was his father, a stern, religious patriarch of the community, a model of or even an incitement to rebellion, for apparently the boy was not averse to religious conformity. In school he excelled in mathematics.

However, like many a youth in the late years of the nineteenth century, Kilpatrick read Darwin's *The Origin of Species* and thought about the truth of the theology of Fundamentalist Christian religion. Like many other youths, Kilpatrick found himself unable to accept the letter of orthodox religion while yearning to retain its spirit. As a junior at Mercer University in Macon, Georgia, he rejected formal religion (Tenenbaum, 1951, pp. 13–14).

The rejection of orthodoxy was to have fateful consequences for Kilpatrick, because after returning to Mercer in 1897 as a teacher of mathematics, he became prominent enough on the faculty to be thought of as its potential president. He served as vice president from 1897 to 1899 and was acting president in

1904. But Mercer was a religiously oriented institution, and in 1906 Kilpatrick resigned after a quasi-public clamor about his religious beliefs or lack of them.

The vocational direction of the man was determined by other factors as well. After graduation from Mercer, Kilpatrick had begun public school teaching at Blakely, Georgia, and like many others attended teachers institutes designed to help classroom teachers. At one such institute in Albany, Georgia, Francis Parker's talk about his Quincy method helped him see a "new vision of education" (Tenenbaum, 1951, p. 26).

Whatever other consequences the resignation from Mercer might have had, the important one is that Kilpatrick did not immediately get another collegiate teaching job and returned to study at Columbia Teachers College in 1907. Why he did this is a long story, but his own experience with public school teaching and a growing unhappiness with the teaching of mathematics were certainly important factors. In 1898 he had attended a summer session at the University of Chicago where he took what he regarded as a "disappointing course" with Dewey. Two years later he had attended another summer session at Cornell University. He took work with Charles DeGarmo, who was using Dewey's *Interest and Effort* as a textbook.

Even as a teacher at Mercer, Kilpatrick was getting more satisfaction out of his nonclassroom experiences with students than from the teaching of mathematics. Tenenbaum (1951, p. 43) quotes him as saying:

> In teaching mathematics, I started out with what I wanted my students to master. . . . I began to perceive that if we wanted rich, meaningful learnings we must start with the student's present knowledge, wishes and interests, whatever they may be and wherever they may lead. . . . They [teachers] began at the wrong place . . . with fixed and set subject matter, when they should have begun with the student's present interests, purposes, abilities, and needs.

Clearly, Kilpatrick's concern was shifting from what was to be taught to how learning takes place. In the first quarter of the twentieth century, Teachers College at Columbia was about the most lively place to pursue and cultivate such an interest.

Far from being disappointed with Dewey's courses, Kilpatrick now became a Dewey disciple at Teachers College. "The work under Dewey remade my philosophy of life and education," Kilpatrick is quoted as saying (Tenenbaum, 1951, p. 75). By 1916 he had the largest enrollment of any teacher at Teachers College. Later he was hailed as the "million dollar" professor because his students had paid over a million dollars in fees to the University. In all, it is estimated that he had 35,000 students, drawn mostly from the ranks of classroom teachers, school principals, and social workers. They came for course credit, but remained quite often to be imbued with a missionary zeal for the formative and redemptive power of education and with a fervent loyalty to the man himself.

There is little doubt, therefore, that Kilpatrick was himself a great teacher and that he had a profound influence on the very people who were doing the work on the front lines of education, in the classroom. The influence of Kilpatrick was extended not only through his highly popular classes but through his articles and books, perhaps by one article in particular, "The Project Method" (Kilpatrick, 1918).

The Project Method

To understand the importance of the project method it is necessary to realize that it proposes to turn the school's back on the mastery of bodies of subject matter such as mathematics, history, geography, and language. The outcomes of schooling are character traits and personality traits.

> The aim and process of teaching as now best conceived differ significantly from what formerly prevailed—and, as we have seen, still largely prevail in high school and college. In the older outlook the almost exclusive teaching emphasis was, and is, on imparting knowledge. In the newer outlook the emphasis is on helping to develop desirable, inclusive character and personality, with especial regard to the dynamic quality of such a character. Does the person being taught grow as a total personality? Does he grow, as a result of the teaching, more sensitive to possibilities inherent in life around him so as to seize upon these fruitfully? Does he grow more

disposed to take hold effectively to bring things to pass? Is he more persistent in his efforts? Does he meanwhile become practically better informed and wiser about such matters as he works with? Does he become more creative in his approach? Does he grow in the tendency to consider thoughtfully what he does? Has he adequate knowledge from present and past with which so to consider? (Kilpatrick, 1951, p. 300).

This passage illustrates better than any commentary can what Kilpatrick thought was the proper order of priorities in formal education. Knowledge, it will be noted, is listed last and only as an instrument or means to character. This outlook reminds us of the Socratic emphasis, but although some of Kilpatrick's followers have likened him to the Athenian dialectician, the comparison is not apt. For the root of the Socratic outlook is that there is an ultimate structure to the moral life that man can discern and study as well as exemplify in his own life, whereas as years went by, Kilpatrick found less and less in life and belief that was ultimate and unchanging. Socrates prodded his students to examine their lives to realize how little they knew, not to have them doubt that there was something fundamental and unchanging to be known.

So far as method of teaching is concerned, Kilpatrick staked everything on "wholeheartedness." Increasingly this became his criterion for teaching: was the pupil wholeheartedly involved in whatever it was he was doing? For him it was certainly a necessary condition for good schooling, and it is perhaps no exaggeration to say that it came to be a sufficient one. The hearty purposeful act was the typical unit of "worthy life." "If we conceive activities as ranging on a scale from those performed under dire compulsion up to those into which one puts his 'whole heart,' the argument herein restricts the term 'project' or purposeful act to the upper portions of the scale" (Kilpatrick, 1918, p. 322).

The purposeful act is regarded not only as the typical unit of the worthy life for the individual but also a unit of worthy life in a democratic society. It follows "that to base education on purposeful acts is exactly to identify the process of education with worthy living itself" (Kilpatrick, 1918, p. 323).

The curriculum, accordingly, becomes a series of tasks suitable to the interests of the pupils. Kilpatrick lists the following types of projects:

1. Where the purpose is to embody some idea in external form, e.g., to present a play or build a boat.
2. Where the purpose is to enjoy some esthetic experience, e.g., listening to a story or a symphony.
3. Where the purpose is to straighten out some intellectual difficulty, i.e., to solve a problem.
4. Where the purpose is to obtain some item or degree of skill or knowledge (Kilpatrick, 1918, pp. 333–334).

Purposing, planning, executing, and judging are the most generalized steps for the teacher to institute. Dewey's problem-solving therefore becomes one special type of project. The other types are less rigorously scientific, but all emphasize the acts of choice, judgment, and commitment, i.e., wholeheartedness.

The other steps of method—presentation, eliciting of the trial response, correcting the trial response, and eliciting the test response—are all present in the Kilpatrick lesson, but they take on distinctive form. The teacher does not present the task so much as he helps the pupil define it, for the task is not to learn something from a book but to fulfill a need or a desire or to relieve a difficulty. Exploration of purposes is therefore part of finding and defining the task. Trial responses and their correction are taken care of in the planning and execution of the chosen goals, whereas the judging phase takes care of the test response. The test is no more and no less than the results of the activity and its efficacy in achieving the goal to which it was directed.

Part of Kilpatrick's faith in so revolutionary a method for schooling was his belief in what he called "concomitant" learnings. Because the child acts as a complete organism in all of its activities, he learns much that is not deliberately being taught to him, and "these sideline learnings are possibly the most significant of all determinants of character" (Kilpatrick, 1951, p. 303). In other words, what one learns is one's attitudes toward what one is learning about and toward learning itself. That this is of prime concern to Kilpatrick is witnessed by the innumerable passages in which he deplores the hatred of school felt by schoolboys down through the generations.

At a time in our culture when emotional adjustment, group living, and moral integrity were being made difficult by lack of community and communal homogeneity, it was important for people to become inner-directed, self-disciplined personalities. It made sense to a whole generation of dedicated teachers to devote the school years to the practice of those activities that people in their adult lives have to enact in the daily round. Compared with this, knowledge of algebra and history, physics and chemistry were of little import, especially when it was thought that most of our people would have little use for such disciplines in their work and life.

The activity classroom, accordingly, was characterized more by discussion, planning, and overt movement and less by reading, telling, and reciting. Pupils learned what they lived, to use a favorite phrase of Kilpatrick's. Thinking for the sake of thinking, theory for the sake of theory, knowledge for the sake of knowledge, had little place in the activity classroom. It stressed intelligence, but it played down intellectualism.

Role of the Teacher

The role of the teacher in the project lesson is summarized by Kilpatrick as follows: The teacher helps (1) to initiate the activity, (2) to plan how to carry the activity forward, (3) to execute the plan, (4) to evaluate progress, (5) to think up and note new leads, (6) to formulate the new leads by writing them down for later recall, (7) keep the pupils critical of their thinking en route to the solution, (8) look back over the whole process to pick up and fix important kinds of learning as well as draw lessons for the future (Kilpatrick, 1951, p. 307).

The discussion techniques developed by Kilpatrick and his pupils not only became familiar in classrooms, but were adopted by other organizations. The breaking up of conferences into small groups that carry on discussion among themselves and with other groups, the "buzz" sessions, and the whole apparatus of recording and reporting these discussions owe much to Kilpatrick.

For the good teacher to operate in the Kilpatrick style he must (a) love children and love to be with them, which is reminiscent of Rousseau and Pestalozzi; (b) know and understand children, their interests and outlooks, an emphasis that also received great stress from Rousseau and Pestalozzi, and which, in turn, gave a great stimulus to the child study movement in modern education; (c) know civilization and the environment in which children live.

The third requirement throws light not only on the method of the activity school but also on its history and justification. If the school was to have a central role in reforming the culture, the teacher would have to know what the culture was like and how it impinged on pupils and their tasks. It was not enough for the teacher to know a subject or even a set of them. Hence during the twenties and even more in the thirties, the social foundations of education were an important ingredient in the training of teachers.

Because Kilpatrick and some other faculty members at Teachers College at Columbia were not enthusiastic about certain features of our society and held that these features were holding back the realization of the democratic dream, they were perceived as radicals of the left. The taint of radicalism was inevitably albeit illogically attached to their educational doctrines so that much of the ensuing controversies about the schools were filled with irrelevancies and nonsense.

In the sixties, under the stress of the Cold War and the high premium put upon science and mathematics by the demands of scientifically based technology, the emphasis on the social orientation of prospective teachers came under attack. It was charged that the educationists had sacrificed the knowledge of the subject to be taught for knowledge about the pupil and opinions about his cultural environment. The latter, they felt, could be dispensed with.

Yet even in the most decorus, subject-matter schools the problems of the cultural impact on the learner cannot be swept under the rug. Culturally deprived children, children with adverse minority status, and the discrepancies between the ground rules for success in the culture and the ideals professed by it cannot be made irrelevant to the teaching-learning transaction. Even when the school cannot and will not do anything directly about such problems, a teacher ignorant of them is a daily victim of cultural naïveté and will never understand why his best efforts are so regularly frustrated.

The activity teacher, finally, has to be able to efface his own purposes and interests in order to make those of the learner central. Although this requirement makes sense, it becomes relevant only when the teacher is no longer regarded as a source of knowledge from which the pupil receives both the content and form of his intellectual life. In a subject-matter curriculum the teacher's mind is a model for that of the pupil's. Ideally, the teacher's knowledge is organized, his language and thinking precise. The pupil, one hopes, will try to imitate the model. The purposes of the teacher and pupil, it is assumed, are identical, and if not, the change is to be effected in the pupil and not in the teacher.

In the activity school, however, the teacher is not a pipeline from the established fields of knowledge, but rather a guide of discussion, planning, executing, and judging. His superiority lies in wider experience and steadier character rather than in intellectual brillance and prowess. In one way, this reduces the demands upon the teacher, because he can have relatively modest intellectual attainments and still do quite well. Even when a pupil knows more than he, there is no stigma to admitting ignorance; indeed, one might turn the situation to advantage in classroom strategy. The teacher is a guide but also a learner and takes pride in this status. On the other hand, the activity teacher needs a lot of what has been called social intelligence, a term that covers everything from tact to a sensitivity to small cues in pupil behavior. The art of self-effacement, therefore, can be as satisfying as self-exhibition, provided the setting is right and the judges know the rules under which the game is being played.

Observations on the Project Method

The fate of the project method was no exception to the general law that operated with other innovations in teaching. Because one could specify steps for the project method, well-intentioned teachers could imitate the form of the method without necessarily adopting its spirit. As a result, the method was often used to sugar-coat the teaching of standard subjects rather than to displace them. The wholeheartedness of the pupil on which Kilpatrick placed so much store was forgotten in the wholeheartedness of the teacher who was determined to have a project on India, or conservation, or whatever it was that her pupils were resisting in history or geography textbooks. The perversion of the project method was perhaps the most common outcome of the activity movement in American education. On the other hand, many teachers caught a bit of the Kilpatrick dedication and simple Pestalozzian belief in the redemptive power of schooling for all children. Somehow, they felt, the American school could and would release the powers of intelligent self-determination in children of all races and creeds and so firmly habituate them in the skills and attitudes of democracy that vested interests, social classes, and intellectual elites would never again subject the common man to superstition and despotism.

Perhaps the most direct challenge to the project method was the teaching of the symbolic skills. Could one really teach reading and the multiplication tables through the indirect project activity? In reply Kilpatrick said: "I will have my primary children *live* reading" (Kilpatrick, 1951, p. 317), and he explained that they will live their reading through the use of bulletin boards for school announcements, accounts of pupil experiences written and read in class. This he believes will motivate the pupil properly for more direct instruction in reading (Kilpatrick, 1951, p. 318). Similarly, the multiplication table becomes "living arithmetic" through the arranging of the proper number of chairs, ordering milk for lunch, giving out supplies, and similar real tasks.

In appraising the project method, one notes that three principles seem to be dominant in it:

1. The project method assumed that the kind of problem-solving involved in large projects would develop general problem-solving skills and that, therefore, practice on large num-

bers of problems related to each principle being studied would be unnecessary (Wallen & Travers, 1963, pp. 497–498).

2. The project method represented a revolt against the use of anxiety as a motive manipulated by the teacher (Wallen & Travers, 1963, p. 497).

3. The project method gave attitudinal learnings priority over cognitive ones.

Of these three principles perhaps the most enduring is the second.

> It seems clear that one major conclusion survives the criticisms . . . that reducing the amount of authoritarian control over students (in some cases rather markedly) does not necessarily result in drastic impairment of their academic skills, contrary to the expectation of many. It seems unlikely, even if one controlled all the possible uncontrolled sources of variation previously discussed which may have worked in favor of the "progressive" schools, that the reduction of authoritarian control would result in a much poorer showing of the "progressive" as compared to the "traditional" students. Certainly it has been demonstrated that many students can and do achieve academically in a less authoritarian school (Wallen & Travers, 1963, p. 474).

Doubts about the first principle are fostered by the amount of noncommon-sense generalizations and knowledge needed to solve all but the most common and gross problems of practical life. Doubts as to the third principle are related to the same situation, namely, that knowledge is no longer regarded as funded information or facts to be remembered but rather as a style of conceptualizing one's experience in terms of theory.

Chapter *XII*

CHALLENGES OLD AND NEW

With the Sophists the Western world achieved a high order of consciousness about the problems of teaching. The Sophists analyzed subject matter into teachable form. In the schools of Rhetoric in Greece and Rome from Isocrates to Quintilian elaborate exercises and precepts for achieving success through eloquence were perfected. This type of teaching achieved its goals by a kind of formalism based on the imitation of models. Although hampered by shortcomings, it had more flexibility than is customarily associated with this approach.

In reaction against teaching virtue through Rhetoric or against the substitution of eloquence for virtue, Socrates tried to teach virtue differently: by inciting the pupil through exhortation and dialogue into a search for the ultimate norms of the Good, the True, and the Beautiful. Socrates saw the teacher as the midwife helping the pupil bring to birth what he had already conceived. Combined with Socrates' emphasis on teaching as a kind of self-examination was Plato's reliance on the study of mathematics and dialectic as the road to true virtue.

This confrontation of the Sophists and Socrates is repeated, with appropriate cultural variations, whenever debates over the primacy of the direct and indirect aspects of educational strategy occur. The Sophists represent the view that the school should aim as directly as possible at the kind of behaviors to be used in adult life, e.g., arguing in courts of law, declaiming at public functions, persuading legislative assemblies, and the like. Socrates represents the view that only by reforming the personality and the cognitive structure of the individual can we achieve the good life; vocational skills albeit important are therefore secondary. The lack of this more general educative influence was felt by Charlemagne even though his courtiers were receiving adequate *ad hoc* training to discharge the demands of war and gallantry. Hence, he called upon Alcuin to restore the rudiments of learning to the clergy and princes of his realm.

In Abelard and Scholasticism the technical resources of formal logic were used to rationalize and intellectualize the creedal and institutional developments of Christianity. In the very process of doing so, Abelard and the Scholastics developed a method of teaching their students to do likewise and in turn to teach others. The medieval disputation was the end product of developments that mingled some of the techniques of the Rhetoricians, the rules of formal logic, and the content of the religious writings of Christianity. One can imagine that when a genuine search for God animated the great debates, the results were as genuine and moving as when Socrates' pupils were animated by genuine yearning for self-discovery; contrariwise when the motivation was merely to display eristic skill, responsible citizens could hardly be blamed for having reservations about what these young men would come to.

The Renaissance presented the schoolman with a new challenge. Instead of having to reconcile Christian theology with Greek logic and science, he now had to cope with a renewed love affair between Western man and classical literature. These literatures celebrated ideals and virtues that did not easily lend themselves to translation in terms of faith, hope, and charity. The conditions for entering the Christian heaven and the pagan heaven were different. The issue became crucial for the prospective governor and courtier, and Roger Ascham proposed a type of education designed to enable its recipients to make the most of both worlds.

The Jesuit schools were discussed as examples of what system and method could achieve when a curriculum devoted to the classical literatures and languages, philosophy, and theology was pressed into the service of the ideal of the Catholic Christian gentleman. They utilized the analytical power of the Rhetoricians to order and present their materials, but in a way that systematized and perfected the art of schoolkeeping. They regularized motivation, testing, and correction, and they did not leave the preparation of teaching to chance.

In Comenius, Pestalozzi, and Froebel, schooling took its cue from the conviction that Nature, having plotted the course of human development, not only biologically, but cognitively and morally as well, could provide a design for teaching. Not only the natural impulses and activities of children, but also the ordinary objects of daily life and the vernacular languages, were the keys to the good life, the good society, and God. So the concrete object, sense perception, usefulness in life, came to be recognized in teaching, but whereas in Comenius and Pestalozzi they were incorporated into the teaching of languages and information about the world, in Froebel the tone of the enterprise changed radically. A metaphysical romanticism in which the child symbolized the unity of all things in God created a spirit that was especially friendly to the kindergarten as an educational institution and child study as discipline.

In Herbart, there was a sophisticated return to the Sophists. Instruction became highly methodized and rationalized. Cognitive elements returned to centrality and affective syndromes were derived from them. It was a new formula for virtue through knowledge, but not through self-knowledge alone and not through the semi-mystical conversion hoped for by Plato, but rather through the orderly building of idea clusters from the intellectual resources of the race. How these idea clusters were to be constructed constituted his theory of method.

Finally, William Heard Kilpatrick was discussed to illustrate the way in which the challenge of taking democracy seriously was met by the schools. This book will close by discussing other challenges that either face the schools now or will do so in the near future.

Why, it may be asked, was so sensible a solution to the problems of mass schooling so short-lived? Why in the space of about 25 years did the activity school and, to a lesser extent, the project method fall into disrepute?

If we have learned anything from our brief survey of teaching methods, it is that the success routes of an era dictate the dominant patterns of schooling and the styles of teaching. Dur-

ing the thirties when America was feeling the effects of World
War I and the great economic depression, and when the
task of making our immigrants literate was pretty well accom-
plished, the roads to success became obscured. Great business
tycoons had demonstrated their fallibility and great statesmen
had made a mess of the peace; even the scientists who had
ushered in the great era of technological progress seemed unable to find ways of utilizing our abundant resources for a better
life. Unemployment and starvation amidst potential plenty pro-
foundly shocked both the intellectual and the common man in
the thirties. Government was the only instrument left to bridge
the gap and solve the paradox.

Group effort translated into political action seemed the only
plausible road to national salvation, so while men continued to
go to school to become doctors, lawyers, and businessmen, it
all seemed like a marking of time until the government restored
a viable economy. In the meantime, the reformers could find re-
ceptive listeners when they argued that the best ideals of democracy had been betrayed by the success figures of the past.
Like Socrates recalling Athenians to the cultivation of virtue,
the Progressive schoolmen issued a call for the cultivation of
genuinely democratic citizenship and a breaking up of the
standard success formula. Since if carried out this would mean
a reshuffling of power and elites, the call no doubt disturbed
those whom it threatened, but to the liberal intellectual it did
make sense.

It also made sense to many a young man and woman with
a rural background whose lives had been restricted by the mores
of the small community and the demands of orthodox religion.
It also made sense to the anti-intellectual strains in our culture
that have always been suspicious of too much book learning and
verbalism. It made sense to many others who found adjustment
to urban life difficult and bewildering. To these people getting
along with others was both a philosophy and a therapy.

Nevertheless, outside of a few schools, many of them pri-
vately operated, the activity movement in its genuine form
found no home. Some of its aura and some of its devices did.
The unit, the project, the whole child, the arousal of effort

through interest, respect for the needs of the child, a revulsion against coercion in instruction—these became part of the common vocabulary, and perhaps even part of the common attitude among professional school people. These effects were accelerated and consolidated by the textbook writers in the field of education, so that successive generations of teachers were nourished on them.

If the movement failed in its central thrust, namely, as a design for curriculum and teaching, it was because no technologically sophisticated mass society can survive without (a) strong intellectual elites to carry on the research requisite for technology, (b) strong engineering and technical cadres to apply the new knowledge to all phases of life, and (c) large numbers of citizens with cognitive and evaluative maps that are theoretical and general enough to enable them to understand and control the social forces within the culture, and the elites to whom they must delegate authority. For such a society, especially if it is to remain free and democratic, wholeheartedness is not enough; not even intelligent wholeheartedness and decency are enough.

Such a society simply does not dare leave the acquisition of systematized knowledge to concomitant learnings, the by-products of projects that are themselves wholesome slices of juvenile life. Intelligence without systematized knowledge will do only for the most ordinary everyday problems. International amity, survival in an atomic age, automation, racial integration are not common everyday problems to which common-sense knowledge and a sense of decency are adequate.

A highly corporate society must have elites in the strategic power positions. The new success routes put a premium on theoretical learnings, on intellectuality as well as intelligence. The schools belatedly but inevitably responded to these pressures. Unfortunately, the challenge to prepare a highly sophisticated citizenry to choose and control the elites democratically has as yet to be met.

We have yet to evolve the teaching method and style appropriate to the new age. The intellectual who can stimulate pupils to think as the best scientists do, who combines the creativity and boldness of the good artist with the self-discipline of the trained scholar, may be the model teacher of the future. Teacher-training programs are in ferment because the teacher demanded by this type of schooling is not the type that teacher-training institutions have been producing. Whether enough of such teachers can ever be produced is itself a question, because brilliant scholars are only infrequently attracted to teaching, especially public school teaching.

As in previous eras, the success routes of the day are already being deplored, and warnings that men will lose their virtue and the ultimate success in life are heard more and more frequently. The humanities valiantly press their claim to wisdom despite their shrinking role *vis-à-vis* science in the shaping of the culture. It would be surprising if from these warnings a method of teaching virtue in these troublesome days did not emerge as a response to the intellectualistic vocationalism of the day. What the model for this type of teaching will be is even more unclear than the model for the success routes, but it probably will not affect the operations of the public schools much for a long time to come.

Whatever models emerge for those who seek the success of the moment or the virtue for long-range success, there will be a few innovators and a host of imitators. The professional educationist, like his ancestors in all periods of history, will reduce the innovation to methodical procedures that can be imitated and taught to prospective teachers. If this saddens those who deplore the exploitation of genius by and for the common man, let them be consoled by the fact that to live, an idea needs a body, and that schools and teachers furnish a kind of body in which educational theory achieves whatever life it enjoys. That the innovation of today will become formalized, dead, and otiose is almost inevitable, but a destiny no more nor less glorious awaits its successors.

References

Abelard, P. *Sic et non.* In V. Cousin, *Ouvrages inédits d'Abélard.* Paris: Imprimérie Royale, 1836.

Abelson, P. *The seven liberal arts.* New York: Teachers Coll., Columbia Univer., 1906.

Ascham, R. *The schoolmaster.* London: Cassell, 1900.

Bacon, F. *The advancement of learning* and *Novum organum.* New York: Colonial Press, 1900.

Broudy, H. S. *Building a philosophy of education.* (2nd ed.) Englewood Cliffs, N.J.: Prentice-Hall, 1961.

Broudy, H. S. Socrates and the teaching machine. *Phi Delta Kappan,* 1963, 44, 243–247.

Brubacher, J. S. *A history of the problems of education.* New York: McGraw-Hill, 1947.

Cicero. *De oratore* and *De partitione oratoria.* Trans. by E. W. Sutton & H. Rackham. London: Heinemann, 1942. 2 vols.

Clark, D. L. Imitation: theory and practice in Roman rhetoric. *Quart. J. Speech,* 1951, 37, 11–22.

Clark, D. L. *Rhetoric in Greco-Roman education.* New York: Columbia Univer. Press, 1957.

Comenius, J. A. *Didactica magna.* In *Opera omnia.* Amsterdam: D. Laurentii de Geer, 1657.

Compayré, G. *Herbart and education by instruction.* Trans. by M. E. Findlay. London: Harrap, 1908. (a)

Compayré, G. *Johann Heinrich Pestalozzi and elementary education.* Trans. by R. P. Jago. London: Harrap, 1908. (b)

Copleston, F. J. *A history of philosophy.* New York: Doubleday, Image Books, 1962. 2 vols.

Cornford, F. M. *The Republic of Plato.* New York: Oxford Univer. Press, 1945.

Craig, R. C. Directed vs. independent discovery of established relations. *J. educ. Psychol.,* 1956, 47, 223–234.

Cubberley, E. P. *The history of education.* Boston: Houghton Mifflin, 1920. (a)

Cubberley, E. P. *Readings in the history of education.* Boston: Houghton Mifflin, 1920. (b)

DeGuimps, R. *Pestalozzi: his life and work.* Trans. by J. Russell. New York: Appleton, 1895.

Dewey, J. *Democracy and education.* New York: Macmillan, 1916.

Dewey, J. *How we think.* Boston: Heath, 1910, 1933.

Dewey, J. Interest as related to the training of the will. *Yearb. National Herbart Soc.*, 1895, 2nd Supp.

Dewey, J. *The quest for certainty.* New York: Minton Balch, 1929.

Dewey, J. *Reconstruction in philosophy.* New York: Holt, 1920.

DeWulf, M. *Philosophy and civilization in the Middle Ages.* New York: Dover, 1922, 1953.

Duckett, Eleanor S. *Alcuin, friend of Charlemagne.* New York: Macmillan, 1951.

Durkheim, E. *Education and sociology.* Trans. by S. D. Fox. Glencoe, Ill.: The Free Press, 1956.

Eby, F., & Arrowood, C. F. *The development of modern education.* New York: Prentice-Hall, 1940.

Elyot, T. *The boke named the gouernour.* Trans. by H. H. S. Croft. London: Kegan Paul, Trench, 1883. 2 vols.

Felkin, H. M., & Felkin, Emmie. *An introduction to Herbart's science and practice of education.* Boston: Heath, 1898.

Fitzpatrick, E. A. *St. Ignatius and the ratio studiorum.* New York: McGraw-Hill, 1933.

Freeman, K. J. *Schools of Hellas.* New York: Macmillan, 1907.

Froebel, F. W. *Autobiography.* Trans. by Emilie Michaelis & H. K. Moore. Syracuse, N.Y.: Bardeen, 1889.

Froebel, F. W. *The education of man.* Trans. by W. N. Hailmann. Internat. Ed. Series, Vol. 5. New York: Appleton, 1911.

Gage, N. L. (Ed.) *Handbook of research on teaching.* Chicago: Rand McNally, 1963.

Gomperz, T. *Greek thinkers.* New York: Scribner, 1901, 1912. 4 vols.

Guilford, J. P. Three faces of intellect. *Amer. Psychologist,* 1959, 14, 469–479.

Harnack, A. *History of dogma.* London: Williams & Norgate, 1896–1899. 7 vols.

Haslerud, G. M., & Meyers, Shirley. The transfer value of given and individually derived principles. *J. educ. Psychol.,* 1958, 49, 293–298.

Hendrix, Gertrude. A new clue to the transfer of training. *Elem. sch. J.,* 1947, 48, 197–208.

Herbart, J. F. *The science of education.* Trans. by H. M. Felkin & Emmie Felkin. Boston: Heath, 1893.

Herbart, J. F. *Letters and lectures on education.* Trans. by H. M. Felkin & Emmie Felkin. Syracuse, N.Y.: Bardeen, 1898.

Isocrates. *Panegyricus, Antidosis, Against the Sophists, Panathenaicus, Areopagiticus,* and *To Philip.* Trans. by G. Norlin. London: Loeb Classical Library, 1929. 3 vols.

Jaeger, W. W. *Paideia: the ideals of Greek culture.* Trans. by G. Highet. New York: Oxford Univer. Press, Vol. I (2nd ed.), 1945; Vol. II, 1943; Vol. III, 1944.

Keatinge, M. W. *The great didactic of John Amos Comenius.* London: Adam and Charles Black, 1896.

Kilpatrick, W. H. The project method. *Teachers Coll. Rec.,* 1918, 319–335.

Kilpatrick, W. H. *Philosophy of education.* New York: Macmillan, 1951.

Krüsi, H. Recollections of my pedagogical life. Stuttgart: 1840. Trans. in Henry Barnard's *American Journal of Education,* 1858, 5, 162–163.

Krüsi, H. *Pestalozzi: his life work, and influence.* New York: American Book, 1857.

Laistner, M. L. W. *Thought and letters in Western Europe, A.D. 500 to 900.* Ithaca, N.Y.: Cornell Univer. Press, 1957.

Marrou, H. I. *Saint Augustin et la fin de la culture antique.* Paris: E. de Boccard, 1938.

Marrou, H. I. *A history of education in antiquity.* Trans. by G. Lamb. New York: Sheed & Ward, 1956.

McKeon, R. Literary criticism and the concept of imitation in antiquity. *Mod. Philol.,* 1936, 34, 1–35.

Moore, E. C. *The story of instruction.* New York: Macmillan, 1936–1938. 2 vols.

Page, R. B. *The letters of Alcuin.* New York: The Forest Press, 1909.

Pestalozzi, J. H. *How Gertrude teaches her children.* Trans. by L. E. Holland & F. C. Turner. Syracuse, N.Y.: Bardeen, 1894.

Plato. *The dialogues of Plato.* Trans. by B. Jowett. (4th ed.) Oxford: Clarendon Press, 1953. 4 vols.

Plato. *Selections.* R. Demos (Ed.) New York: Scribner, 1927.

Quintilian, F. B. *Institutio oratoria.* Trans. by H. E. Butler. Cambridge, Mass.: Harvard Univer. Press, 1953. 4 vols.

Rashdall, H. *The universities of Europe in the Middle Ages.* F. M. Powicke & A. B. Emden (Eds.) Oxford: Clarendon, 1936. 3 vols.

Sikes, J. G. *Peter Abailard.* Cambridge: Cambridge Univer. Press, 1932.

Silber, K. *Pestalozzi, the man and his work.* London: Routledge and Kegan Paul, 1960.

Smith, B. O. A concept of teaching. *Teachers Coll. Rec.,* 1960, 61, 229–241.

Smith, B. O., & Ennis, R. H. (Eds.) *Language and concepts in education.* Chicago: Rand McNally, 1961.

Spinka, M. *John Amos Comenius: that incomparable Moravian.* Chicago: Univer. of Chicago Press, 1943.

Tenenbaum, S. *William Heard Kilpatrick: trail blazer in education.* New York: Harper, 1951.

Ulich, R. *Three thousand years of educational wisdom.* (2nd ed.) Cambridge, Mass.: Harvard Univer. Press, 1954.

Wallen, N. E., & Travers, R. M. W. Analysis and investigation in teaching methods. In N. L. Gage (Ed.), *Handbook of research on teaching.* Chicago: Rand McNally, 1963. Pp. 448–505.

Winterton, F. The lesson of neo-scholasticism. *Mind,* 1888, 13, 398–400.

Index